The Dictionary of Legal Bullshit

Randall C. Young

SPHINX PUBLISHING
AN IMPRINT OF SOURCEBOOKS, INC®
NAPERVILLE, ILLINOIS

First Edition: 2007

Published by: Sphinx® Publishing, An Imprint of Sourcebooks, Inc.®
Naperville Office
P.O. Box 4410
Naperville, Illinois 60567-4410
630-961-3900
Fax: 630-961-2168
www.sourcebooks.com
www.SphinxLegal.com

This publication is designed to provide accurate and authoritative information in regard to the subject matter covered. It is sold with the understanding that the publisher is not engaged in rendering legal, accounting, or other professional service. If legal advice or other expert assistance is required, the services of a competent professional person should be sought.

From a Declaration of Principles Jointly Adopted by a Committee of the American Bar Association and a Committee of Publishers and Associations.

This product is not a substitute for legal advice.
Disclaimer required by Texas statutes.

Library of Congress Cataloging-in-Publication Data
Young, Randall C.
 The dictionary of legal bullshit / by Randall C. Young. -- 1st ed.
   p. cm.
 ISBN-13: 978-1-57248-636-2 (pbk. : alk. paper)
 ISBN-10: 1-57248-636-8 (pbk. : alk. paper) 1. Law--United States--Terminology--Humor. 2. Lawyers--United States--Humor. 3. Practice of law--United States--Humor. I. Title.

K184.Y68 2007
340.01'4--dc22

                                        2007023926

Printed and bound in the United States of America.
VP — 10 9 8 7 6 5 4 3 2 1

To my wife, Patricia, who tolerates
most of my B.S.

debt • bait and switch • bankrupt • bankruptcy •bar •bar review course • basis • bench • best evidence rule • big gun •bilious •billable hour •birdie •black a
ck letter law • blue book • bogart • bogie • boiler plate • bonus • book •boot •booty • bork • bribe • bust •busted • c.a.f.o. •calendar call • chain • child sup
rning the file • circumstantial evidence •citation • class action • clearly • clients • closing costs • coffee • comparative negligence • compensatory damage
deration • constitutional law • contract • contributory negligence • contumacious • corporation • corpus delicti • counselor • creditor • cross examination • dead
d man's acts • deceit • deep pocket • de minimis non curat lex • demurrer • deposition • derogatory clause • devil's dictionary • dictionary, law • directed ver
closure • divorce • dormant commerce clause • dorr's Rebellion • double billing • double jeopardy • due process • dying declaration • e.s.o.p. employee share ow
plan • eagle • economic development program • ego • eighth amendment •ejuration • entitlement • equal protection clause • equity • escheat •estate • esto
pel, equitable • ethics • evidence, laws of / rules of • excited utterance • exclusionary rule • exculpatory evidence rule • exhaustion of remedies • ex-wife
and • face time • fair • fair use doctrine • fairway • false arrest • federal judge • federalism • federalism • federal witness protection program • federalist soc
h amendment • fifteenth amendment • filibuster • first amendment • floating crap game • fourteenth amendment • fourth amendment • force majeure • fran
age •fraud • frivolous • fruit of the poisonous tree • fundamental right • garden • general denial • gerrymander • gift causa mortis • gift tax • gloss • good sam
tatues • got my papers! • great compromise • graft • gross • guarantee clause • guilt • h.a.p. • habeas corpus • habitability • habitability, warrantee of • har
Learned • harmless error • harvard law • hassle • hazardous • hazardous waste • headnote • hearsay • heirloom • hereinabove, hereinafter, heretofore • he s
aid • homicide • hornbook • hose • hundred weight • hung jury • ill fame • immoral • impediment to marriage • import-export clause • imputed negligence • impe
orporation by reference • income • inchoate • indemnity • indigent • inevitable discovery rule • infancy • internal Revenue code • internal Revenue service • in
al property • interstate commerce • ipso facto • irrelevant • jack • jeopardy • judicial review • jump • jail • jailhouse lawyer • joint and several liability • journal
age • judgment • judgment not withstanding the verdict • jurisprudence • jury • jury instructions • jury wheel • just compensation • justice • justification • k.
ver-cellars act • kentucky rule • kick • kickback • kilo • kiting • kleptomania • knock and announce • know • know-it-all • known-heirs • laches, estoppel by •
act • lapse in judgement • law • law of the case • law review • lawyer's trust account • lead counsel • legislative intent • liability • libel • link • liquidated dama
gation • loaded • long-arm jurisdiction • lose • maintenance • malice aforethought • malicious prosecution • malpractice insurance • manual labor • making a rec
riage • marrone • mason • matlock, ben • maundering • mcnaughton Rule • mendacity • mens rea • merely • minnesota twins, the • monopoly • mortgage in
• multi-state • navigable waters • negligence • new york • new york lawyers • ninth amendment • no-knock warrant • not-for-profit corporation • nutshell • ot
n • objection • obscenity • offer • old bailey • oligarchy • originalist • paternity • paternity test • palimony • penultimate • perspicuity • pike test • plea bar
ssey v ferguson • potter, stewart • poverty law • pornography • prevarication • product liability • professional responsibility • prior inconsistent statement • p
aint • prolix • public interest law • public interest lawyer • punitive damages • quantum meruit • quash • quarter section • question presented • quid pro quo • c
deed • rainmaker • rational basis test • rejection • remand • residuum • residuum rule • res ipsa loquitor • res judicata • respondent superior • responsible off
• rule against perpetuities • screw • screw-the-pooch • second amendment • sentence • separation of powers • settlement • seventh amendment • sinking fur
enth amendment • sixth amendment • slander • solicitation • spendthrift • stare decisis • stages of marriage • statute • statutes of frauds • street lawyer • s
ruction • strict scrutiny • sub rosa • substantive due process • sudden heat of passion • summer associate • taylor law • take it upstairs • taxation • tenth ame
• think-they-know-it-all • third amendment • tickle • title insurance • tort • to wit • traduce • trespass • trust • ultimate • unambiguous • unconstitutional • unif
nmercial code • unique • united states supreme court • unjust enrichment • usury • usufruct • vagrant • verified pleading • very • waiver • waver • warhorse • warra
ss • warranty, implied • warranty period • ways-and-means • webster, daniel • west publishing • whole-life insurance • wirt, william • withholding • yield • y
el • zealous representation • zone of interest test • zoning • absence of malice • accessory • accomplice • acquit • act of god • action • activist judge • actus
ninistrative law • admiralty law • agent • albatross • alimony • alternative pleading • amnesty • ambulance chaser • antitrust laws • appeal • arbitrary and ca
• armed and dangerous • as is • assumpsit • attorney • b.m.w. • bad debt • bait and switch • bankrupt • bankruptcy •bar •bar review course • basis • bene
evidence rule • big gun •bilious •billable hour •birdie •black acre • black letter law • blue book • bogart • bogie • boiler plate • bonus • book •boot •booty •
le • bust •busted • c.a.f.o. •calendar call • chain • child support •churning the file • circumstantial evidence •citation • class action • clearly • clients • clo
• coffee • comparative negligence • compensatory damages • consideration • constitutional law • contract • contributory negligence • contumacious •corp
• corpus delicti • counselor • creditor • cross examination • dead file • dead man's acts • deceit • deep pocket • de minimis non curat lex • demurrer • deposi
gatory clause • devil's dictionary • dictionary, law • directed verdict • disclosure • divorce • dormant commerce clause • dorr's Rebellion • double billing • do
rdy • due process • dying declaration • e.s.o.p. employee share ownership plan • eagle absence of malice • accessory • accomplice • acquit • act of god • ac
vist judge • actus reus • administrative law • admiralty law • agent • albatross • alimony • alternative pleading • amnesty • ambulance chaser • antitrust law
al • arbitrary and capricious • armed and dangerous • as is • assumpsit • attorney • b.m.w. • bad debt • bait and switch • bankrupt • bankruptcy •bar • bar revi
e • basis • bench • best evidence rule • big gun •bilious •billable hour •birdie •black acre • black letter law • blue book • bogart • bogie • boiler plate • bonu
•boot •booty • bork • bribe • bust •busted • c.a.f.o. •calendar call • chain • child support •churning the file • circumstantial evidence •citation • class actio
y • clients • closing costs • coffee • comparative negligence • compensatory damages • consideration • constitutional law • contract • contributory negligence
macious •corporation • corpus delicti • counselor • creditor • cross examination • dead file • dead man's acts • deceit • deep pocket • de minimis non curat le
rrer • deposition • derogatory clause • devil's dictionary • dictionary, law • directed verdict • disclosure • divorce • dormant commerce clause • dorr's Rebellio
e billing • double jeopardy • due process • dying declaration • e.s.o.p. employee share ownership plan • eagle • economic development program • ego • eig
dment •ejuration • entitlement • equal protection clause • equity • escheat •estate • estop • estoppel, equitable • ethics • evidence, laws of / rules of • exc
ance • exclusionary rule • exculpatory evidence rule • exhaustion of remedies • ex-wife/ex-husband • face time • fair • fair use doctrine • fairway • false arre
al judge • federalism • federal witness protection program • federalist society • fifth amendment • filibuster • first amendment • floating crap game • fourtee
dment • fourth amendment • force majeure • franking privilege •fraud • frivolous • fruit of the poisonous tree • fundamental right • garden • general denial • ge
er • gift causa mortis • gift tax • gloss • good samaritan statues • got my papers! • great compromise • graft • gross • guarantee clause • guilt • h.a.p. • hab
s • habitability • habitability, warrantee of • hack • hand, Learned • harmless error • harvard law • hassle • hazardous • hazardous waste • headnote • hearsa

Contents

debt • bait and switch • bankrupt • bankruptcy •bar •bar review course • basis • bench • best evidence rule • big gun •bilious •billable hour •birdie •black
lck letter law • blue book • bogart • bogie • boiler plate • bonus • book •boot •booty • bork •bribe • bust •busted • c.a.f.o. •calendar call • chain • child su
rning the file • circumstantial evidence •citation • class action • clearly • clients • closing costs • coffee • comparative negligence • compensatory damag
ideration • constitutional law • contract • contributory negligence • contumacious •corporation • corpus delicti • counselor • creditor • cross examination • dea
ad man's acts • deceit • deep pocket • de minimis non curat lex • demurrer • deposition • derogatory clause • devil's dictionary • dictionary, law • directed ve
closure • divorce • dormant commerce clause • dorr's Rebellion • double billing • double jeopardy • due process • dying declaration • e.s.o.p. employee share ov
plan • eagle • economic development program • ego • eighth amendment •ejuration • entitlement • equal protection clause • equity • escheat •estate • est
ppel, equitable • ethics • evidence, laws of / rules of • excited utterance • exclusionary rule • exculpatory evidence rule • exhaustion of remedies • ex-wife
and • face time • fair • fair use doctrine • fairway • false arrest • federal judge • federalism • federalism • federal witness protection program • federalist so
h amendment • fifteenth amendment • filibuster • first amendment • floating crap game • fourteenth amendment • fourth amendment • force majeure • frar
ege •fraud • frivolous • fruit of the poisonous tree • fundamental right • garden • general denial • gerrymander • gift causa mortis • gift tax • gloss • good sa
statutes • got my papers! • great compromise • graft • gross • guarantee clause • guilt • h.a.p. • habeas corpus • habitability • habitability, warrantee of • he
, Learned • harmless error • harvard law • hassle • hazardous • hazardous waste • headnote • hearsay • heirloom • hereinabove, hereinafter, heretofore • he
said • homicide • hornbook • hose • hundred weight • hung jury • ill fame • immoral • impediment to marriage • import-export clause • imputed negligence • imp
orporation by reference • income • inchoate • indemnity • indigent • inevitable discovery rule • infancy • internal Revenue code • internal Revenue service • i
al property • interstate commerce • ipso facto • irrelevant • jack • jeopardy • judicial review • jump • jail • jailhouse lawyer • joint and several liability • journa
ege • judgment • judgment not withstanding the verdict • jurisprudence • jury • jury instructions • jury wheel • just compensation • justice • justification • k.
uver-cellars act • kentucky rule • kick • kickback • kilo • kiting • kleptomania • knock and announce • know • know-it-all • known-heirs • laches, estoppel by •
act • lapse in judgement • law • law of the case • law review • lawyer's trust account • lead counsel • legislative intent • liability • libel • link • liquidated dam
igation • loaded • long-arm jurisdiction • lose • maintenance • malice aforethought • malicious prosecution • malpractice insurance • manual labor • making a re
irriage • marrone • mason • matlock, ben • maundering • mcnaughton Rule • mendacity • mens rea • merely • minnesota twins, the • monopoly • mortgage in
• multi-state • navigable waters • negligence • new york • new york lawyers • ninth amendment • no-knock warrant • not-for-profit corporation • nutshell • o
m • objection • obscenity • offer • old bailey • oligarchy • originalist • paternity • paternity test • palimony • penultimate • perspicuity • pike test • plea ba
ssey v ferguson • potter, stewart • poverty law • pornography • prevarication • product liability • professional responsibility • prior inconsistent statement •
oint • prolix • public interest law • public interest lawyer • punitive damages • quantum meruit • quash • quarter section • question presented • quid pro quo •
n deed • rainmaker • rational basis test • rejection • remand • residuum • residuum rule • res ipsa loquitor • res judicata • respondent superior • responsible of
• rule against perpetuities • screw • screw-the-pooch • second amendment • sentence • separation of powers • settlement • seventh amendment • sinking fu
enth amendment • sixth amendment • slander • solicitation • spendthrift • stare decisis • stages of marriage • statute • statutes of frauds • street lawyer • s
truction • strict scrutiny • sub rosa • substantive due process • sudden heat of passion • summer associate • taylor law • take it upstairs • taxation • tenth am
• think-they-know-it-all • third amendment • tickle • title insurance • tort • to wit • traduce • trespass • trust • ultimate • unambiguous • unconstitutional • uni
nercial code • unique • united states supreme court • unjust enrichment • usury • usufruct • vagrant • verified pleading • very • waiver • warhorse • warr
ass • warranty, implied • warranty period • ways-and-means • webster, daniel • west publishing • whole-life insurance • wirt, william • withholding • yield • v
kel • zealous representation • zone of interest test • zoning • absence of malice • accessory • accomplice • acquit • act of god • action • activist judge • actus
ministrative law • admiralty law • agent • albatross • alimony • alternative pleading • amnesty • ambulance chaser • antitrust laws • appeal • arbitrary and c
s • armed and dangerous • as is • assumpsit • attorney • b.m.w. • bad debt • bait and switch • bankrupt • bankruptcy •bar •bar review course • basis • ber
evidence rule • big gun •bilious •billable hour •birdie •black acre • black letter law • blue book • bogart • bogie • boiler plate • bonus • book •boot •booty •
pe • bust •busted • c.a.f.o. •calendar call • chain • child support •churning the file • circumstantial evidence •citation • class action • clearly • clients • clo
s • coffee • comparative negligence • compensatorY damages • consideration • constitutional law • contract • contributory negligence • contumacious •corp
• corpus delicti • counselor • creditor • cross examination • dead file • dead man's acts • deceit • deep pocket • de minimis non curat lex • demurrer • depos
rogatory clause • devil's dictionary • dictionary, law • directed verdict • disclosure • divorce • dormant commerce clause • dorr's Rebellion • double billing • do
ardy • due process • dying declaration • e.s.o.p. employee share ownership plan • eagle absence of malice • accessory • accomplice • acquit • act of god • a
ivist judge • actus reus • administrative law • admiralty law • agent • albatross • alimony • alternative pleading • amnesty • ambulance chaser • antitrust law
al • arbitrary and capricious • armed and dangerous • as is • assumpsit • attorney • b.m.w. • bad debt • bait and switch • bankrupt • bankruptcy •bar •bar re
se • basis • bench • best evidence rule • big gun •bilious •billable hour •birdie •black acre • black letter law • blue book • bogart • bogie • boiler plate • bor
•boot •booty • bork •bribe • bust •busted • c.a f.o. •calendar call • chain • child support •churning the file • circumstantial evidence •citation • class acti
ly • clients • closing costs • coffee • comparative negligence • compensatory damages • consideration • constitutional law • contract • contributory negliger
umacious •corporation • corpus delicti • counselor • creditor • cross examination • dead file • dead man's acts • deceit • deep pocket • de minimis non curat
urrer • deposition • derogatory clause • devil's dictionary • dictionary, law • directed verdict • disclosure • divorce • dormant commerce clause • dorr's Rebelli
ile billing • double jeopardy • due process • dying declaration • e.s.o.p. employee share ownership plan • eagle • economic development program • ego • e
ndment •ejuration • entitlement • equal protection clause • equity • escheat •estate • estop • estoppel, equitable • ethics • evidence, laws of / rules of • ex
ance • exclusionary rule • exculpatory evidence rule • exhaustion of remedies • ex-wife/ex-husband • face time • fair • fair use doctrine • fairway • false arre
ral judge • federalism • federal witness protection program • federalist society • fifth amendment • filibuster • first amendment • floating crap game • fourte
ndment • fourth amendment • force majeure • franking privilege •fraud • frivolous • fruit of the poisonous tree • fundamental right • garden • general denial • g
der • • gift causa mortis • gift tax • gloss • good samaritan statues • got my papers! • great compromise • graft • gross • guarantee clause • guilt • h.a.p. • h
us • habitability, warrantee of • hack • hand. Learned • harmless error • harvard law • hassle • hazardous • hazardous waste • headnote • hears

introduction

Bullshit is everywhere in our society. Legal B.S. is particularly insidious because lawyers and judges invest it with the trappings of intellectual abstraction and institutional legitimacy. We buttress it with reams of superfluous writing so nobody has the endurance to parse out the essential meaning or hidden implications of most legal B.S. We probably do this to make ourselves feel important. Most people enjoy feeling smarter than the next guy, and we all like to know things that other people don't know.

Another reason for the high volume of bullshit in law might have something to do with an innate sense of inferiority or insecurity. After all, doctors, engineers, architects, and tradespeople such as welders, plumbers, and mechanics have special skills that set them apart from everyone else. Nobody, or at least very few people, just pick up a lancet and perform a biopsy or grab a wrench and replace a bad u-joint.

By contrast, the lawyer's stock and trade are words—words in contracts, words in pleadings, words in letters, words in court. We read, talk, and write on behalf of people. That's about it. How many people can't read, talk, or write? Okay, maybe that's a bad question. How many people who have the money to hire lawyers can't read, talk, or write?

So, the only ways to justify our phony-baloney jobs are to make what we write so esoteric that only we can understand it and to make ourselves appear to be intellectually superior. The two activities go hand in hand.

Most people would fall into a catatonic state if they had to comb out the exact meanings and consequences of even a simple contract. Law school, like boot camp, is largely about rigorous conditioning that enables graduates to endure things no normal human can withstand. That is why lawyers can charge people outlandish sums of money just to read and write on their behalf.

Sometimes bullshit has its place. Spread liberally and tilled into fields, it returns nutrients to the soil and increases crop yields. Dumped on your lawn, it's just a foul mess.

Unfortunately, when it comes to spreading legal B.S., a lot of lawyers can't distinguish between wide verdant fields and their neighbor's yard. Consider this letter that a law office actually sent to pay for copies of some documents.

Dear Mr. M_____:

Enclosed herein please find our draft in the amount of $74.25, said draft being served upon you in pre-payment for copies of records pertaining to the above referenced . . . [matter].

A normal person would have written:

Dear Mr. M _____:

Thank you for your note about the records we requested regarding project X. I have enclosed a check for $74.25 to pay your fee for copying the documents. Please send them as soon as possible. Thank you for your help.

The official source for most legal bullshit is the law dictionary. Interestingly, a large number of the words in legal dictionaries are the same as words found in standard English dictionaries. The purpose of the law dictionary is to explain how the legal profession has distorted or perverted the meaning of a perfectly ordinary word. Lawyers call such words "terms of art." Normal people might call them bullshit.

Many words commonly used in the legal profession are omitted from the standard law dictionaries because writing down the course and common parlance of lawyers might shatter the carefully crafted persona of seriousness and intellectual superiority that lawyers project to the public at large.

The complex decisions printed in the case reporters contain more than a little in the way of run-on sentences, citations, and footnotes. No lawyer has failed to read at least one decision and exclaim, "oh, that's bullshit!" Few have ever had the courage to say that to the judge who wrote it.

None of that has anything to do with this book.

d debt • bait and switch • bankrupt • bankruptcy •bar •bar review course • basis • bench • best evidence rule • big gun •bilious •billable hour •birdie •black
ack letter law • blue book • bogart • bogie • boiler plate • bonus • book •boot •booty • bork •bribe • bust • busted • c.a.f.o. •calendar call • chain • child su
uming the file • circumstantial evidence •citation • class action • clearly • clients • closing costs • coffee • comparative negligence • compensatory dama
sideration • constitutional law • contract • contributory negligence • contumacious •corporation • corpus delicti • counselor • creditor • cross examination • dea
ad man's acts • deceit • deep pocket • de minimis non curat lex • demurrer • deposition • derogatory clause • devil's dictionary • dictionary, law • directed ve
sclosure • divorce • dormant commerce clause • dorr's Rebellion • double billing • double jeopardy • due process • dying declaration • e.s.o.p. employee share ow
plan • eagle • economic development program • ego • eighth amendment •ejuration • entitlement • equal protection clause • equity • escheat •estate • es
ppel, equitable • ethics • evidence, laws of / rules of • excited utterance • exclusionary rule • exculpatory evidence rule • exhaustion of remedies • ex-wif
band • face time • fair • fair use doctrine • fairway • false arrest • federal judge • federalism • federalism • federal witness protection program • federalist s
th amendment • fifteenth amendment • filibuster • first amendment • floating crap game • fourteenth amendment • fourth amendment • force majeure • fra
lege • fraud • frivolous • fruit of the poisonous tree • fundamental right • garden • general denial • gerrymander • gift causa mortis • gift tax • gloss • good s
statues • got my papers! • great compromise • graft • gross • guarantee clause • guilt • h.a.p. • habeas corpus • habitability • habitability, warrantee of • h
d, Learned • harmless error • harvard law • hassle • hazardous • hazardous waste • headnote • hearsay • heirloom • hereinabove, hereinafter, heretofore • h
said • homicide • hornbook • hose • hundred weight • hung jury • ill fame • immoral • impediment to marriage • import-export clause • imputed negligence • imp
incorporation by reference • income • inchoate • indemnity • indigent • inevitable discovery rule • infancy • internal Revenue code • internal Revenue service •
ual property • interstate commerce • ipso facto • irrelevant • jack • jeopardy • judicial review • jump • jail • jailhouse lawyer • joint and several liability • journ
lege • judgment • judgment not withstanding the verdict • jurisprudence • jury • jury instructions • jury wheel • just compensation • justice • justification • k
uver-cellars act • kentucky rule • kick • kickback • kilo • kiting • kleptomania • knock and announce • know • know-it-all • known-heirs • laches. estopped by •
tract • lapse in judgement • law • law of the case • law review • lawyer's trust account • lead counsel • legislative intent • liability • libel • link • liquidated dam
igation • loaded • long-arm jurisdiction • lose • maintenance • malice aforethought • malicious prosecution • malpractice insurance • manual labor • making a ri
amage • marrone • mason • matlock, ben • maundering • mcnaughton Rule • mendacity • mens rea • merely • minnesota twins, the • monopoly • mortgage
e • multi-state • navigable waters • negligence • new york • new york lawyers • ninth amendment • no-knock warrant • not-for-profit corporation • nutshell •
um • objection • obscenity • offer • old bailey • oligarchy • originalist • paternity • paternity test • palimony • penultimate • perspicuity • pike test • plea ba
essey v. ferguson • potter, stewart • poverty law • pornography • prevarication • product liability • professional responsibility • prior inconsistent statement •
raint • prolix • public interest law • public interest lawyer • punitive damages • quantum meruit • quash • quarter session • question presented • quid pro quo •
m deed • rainmaker • rational basis test • rejection • remand • residuum • residuum rule • res ipsa loquitor • res judicata • respondent superior • responsible c
• rule against perpetuities • screw • screw-the-pooch • second amendment • sentence • separation of powers • settlement • seventh amendment • sinking f
eenth amendment • sixth amendment • slander • solicitation • spendthrift • stare decisis • stages of marriage • statute • statutes of frauds • street lawyer •
struction • strict scrutiny • sub rosa • substantive due process • sudden heat of passion • summer associate • taylor law • take it upstairs • taxation • tenth a
nt • think-they-know-it-all • third amendment • tickle • title insurance • tort • to wit • traduce • trespass • trust • ultimate • unambiguous • unconstitutional • un
mmercial code • unique • united states supreme court • unjust enrichment • usury • usufruct • vagrant • verified pleading • very • waiver • warhorse • war
ress • warranty, implied • warranty period • ways-and-means • webster, daniel • west publishing • whole-life insurance • wirt, william • withholding • yield •
nkel • zealous representation • zone of interest test • zoning • absence of malice • accessory • accomplice • acquit • act of god • action • activist judge • actus
ministrative law • admiralty law • agent • albatross • alimony • alternative pleading • amnesty • ambulance chaser • antitrust laws • appeal • arbitrary and
s • armed and dangerous • as is • assumpsit • attorney • b.m.w. • bad debt • bait and switch • bankrupt • bankruptcy •bar •bar review course • basis • be
t evidence rule • big gun •bilious •billable hour •birdie •black acre • black letter law • blue book • bogart • bogie • boiler plate • bonus • book •boot •booty •
be • bust •busted • c.a.f.o. •calendar call • chain • child support •churning the file • circumstantial evidence •citation • class action • clearly • clients • cl
ts • coffee • comparative negligence • compensatory damages • consideration • constitutional law • contract • contributory negligence • contumacious •cor
• corpus delicti • counselor • creditor • cross examination • dead file • dead man's acts • deceit • deep pocket • de minimis non curat lex • demurrer • depo
erogatory clause • devil's dictionary • dictionary, law • directed verdict • disclosure • divorce • dormant commerce clause • dorr's Rebellion • double billing • d
pardy • due process • dying declaration • e.s.o.p. employee share ownership plan • eagle absence of malice • accessory • accomplice • acquit • act of god • a
ctivist judge • actus reus • administrative law • admiralty law • agent • albatross • alimony • alternative pleading • amnesty • ambulance chaser • antitrust la
eal • arbitrary and capricious • armed and dangerous • as is • assumpsit • attorney • b.m.w. • bad debt • bait and switch • bankrupt • bankruptcy •bar •bar n
rse • basis • bench • best evidence rule • big gun •bilious •billable hour •birdie •black acre • black letter law • blue book • bogart • bogie • boiler plate • bo
k •boot •booty • bork •bribe • bust •busted • c.a.f.o. •calendar call • chain • child support •churning the file • circumstantial evidence •citation • class ac
rly • clients • closing costs • coffee • comparative negligence • compensatory damages • consideration • constitutional law • contract • contributory
tumacious •corporation • corpus delicti • counselor • creditor • cross examination • dead file • dead man's acts • deceit • deep pocket • de minimis non curat
rurrer • deposition • derogatory clause • devil's dictionary • dictionary, law • directed verdict • disclosure • divorce • dormant commerce clause • dorr's Rebel
ble billing • double jeopardy • due process • dying declaration • e.s.o.p. employee share ownership plan • eagle • economic development program • ego •
endment •ejuration • entitlement • equal protection clause • equity • escheat •estate • estop • estoppel, equitable • ethics • evidence, laws of / rules of • e
rance • exclusionary rule • exculpatory evidence rule • exhaustion of remedies • ex-wife/ex-husband • face time • fair • fair use doctrine • fairway • false ar
eral judge • federalism • federal witness protection program • federalist society • fifth amendment • filibuster • first amendment • floating crap game • fourt
endment • fourth amendment • force majeure • franking privilege •fraud • frivolous • fruit of the poisonous tree • fundamental right • garden • general denial •
nder • gift causa mortis • gift tax • gloss • good samaritan statues • got my papers! • great compromise • graft • gross • guarantee clause • guilt • h.a.p. • h
ous • habitability • habitability, warrantee of • hack • hand, Learned • harmless error • harvard law • hassle • hazardous • hazardous waste • headnote • hea

DEFINITIONS SPONSORED BY:

SLAUGHTER, ENGLISH & BABBLE
COUNSELORS AT LAW
SPECIALIZING IN APPELLATE LITIGATION

debt • bait and switch • bankrupt • bankruptcy •bar •bar review course • basis • bench • best evidence rule • big gun •bilious •billable hour •birdie •black

k letter law • blue book • bogart • bogie • boiler plate • bonus • book •boot •booty • bork •bribe • bust •busted • c.a.f.o. •calendar call • chain • child sup

ning the file • circumstantial evidence •citation • class action • clearly • clients • closing costs • coffee • comparative negligence • compensatory damage

feration • constitutional law • contract • contributory negligence • contumacious •corporation • corpus delicti • counselor • creditor • cross examination • dead

d man's acts • deceit • deep pocket • de minimis non curat lex • demurrer • deposition • derogatory clause • devil's dictionary • dictionary, law • directed ver

losure • divorce • dormant commerce clause • dorr's Rebellion • double billing • double jeopardy • due process • dying declaration • e.s o.p. employee share ow

lan • eagle • economic development program • ego • eighth amendment •ejuration • entitlement • equal protection clause • equity • escheat •estate • este

pel, equitable • ethics • evidence, laws of / rules of • excited utterance • exclusionary rule • exculpatory evidence rule • exhaustion of remedies • ex-wife

nd • face time • fair • fair use doctrine • fairway • false arrest • federal judge • federalism • federalism • federal witness protection program • federalist soc

amendment • fifteenth amendment • filibuster • first amendment • floating crap game • fourteenth amendment • fourth amendment • force majeure • fran

ge •fraud • frivolous • fruit of the poisonous tree • fundamental right • garden • general denial • gerrymander • gift causa mortis • gift tax • gloss • good sar

tatues • got my papers! • great compromise • graft • gross • guarantee clause • guilt • h a p. • habeas corpus • habitability • habitability, warrantee of • ha

Learned • harmless error • harvard law • hassle • hazardous • hazardous waste • headnote • hearsay • heirloom • hereinabove, hereinafter, heretofore • he s

aid • homicide • hornbook • hose • hundred weight • hung jury • ill fame • immoral • impediment to marriage • import-export clause • imputed negligence • impe

rporation by reference • income • inchoate • indemnity • indigent • inevitable discovery rule • infancy • internal Revenue code • internal Revenue service • in

l property • interstate commerce • ipso facto • irrelevant • jack • jeopardy • judicial review • jump • jail • jailhouse lawyer • joint and several liability • journal

ge • judgment • judgment not withstanding the verdict • jurisprudence • jury • jury instructions • jury wheel • just compensation • justice • justification • k

ver-cellars act • kentucky rule • kick • kickback • kilo • kiting • kleptomania • knock and announce • know • know-it-all • known-heirs • laches, estoppel by • li

act • lapse in judgement • law • law of the case • law review • lawyer's trust account • lead counsel • legislative intent • liability • libel • link • liquidated dama

ation • loaded • long-arm jurisdiction • lose • maintenance • malice aforethought • malicious prosecution • malpractice insurance • manual labor • making a rec

riage • marrone • mason • matlock, ben • maundering • mcnaughton Rule • mendacity • mens rea • merely • minnesota twins, the • monopoly • mortgage in

• multi-state • navigable waters • negligence • new york • new york lawyers • ninth amendment • no-knock warrant • not-for-profit corporation • nutshell • ob

h • objection • obscenity • offer • old bailey • oligarchy • originalist • paternity • paternity test • palimony • penultimate • perspicuity • pike test • plea bar

sey v. ferguson • potter, stewart • poverty law • pornography • prevarication • product liability • professional responsibility • prior inconsistent statement • p

int • prolix • public interest law • public interest lawyer • punitive damages • quantum meruit • quash • quarter section • question presented • quid pro quo • c

deed • rainmaker • rational basis test • rejection • remand • residuum • residuum rule • res ipsa loqutor • res judicata • respondent superior • responsible for

rule against perpetuities • screw • screw-the-pooch • second amendment • sentence • separation of powers • settlement • seventh amendment • sinking fur

nth amendment • sixth amendment • slander • solicitation • spendthrift • stare decisis • stages of marriage • statute • statutes of frauds • street lawyer • s

uction • strict scrutiny • sub rosa • substantive due process • sudden heat of passion • summer associate • taylor law • take it upstairs • taxation • tenth ame

• think-they-know-it-all • third amendment • tickle • title insurance • tort • to wit • traduce • trespass • trust • ultimate • unambiguous • unconstitutional • unife

ercial code • unique • united states supreme court • unjust enrichment • usury • usufruct • vagrant • verified pleading • very • waiver • warhorse • warran

ss • warranty, implied • warranty period • ways-and-means • webster, daniel • west publishing • whole-life insurance • writ, william • withholding • yield • y

el • zealous representation • zone of interest test • zoning • absence of malice • accessory • accomplice • acquit • act of god • action • activist judge • actus r

inistrative law • admiralty law • agent • albatross • alimony • alternative pleading • amnesty • ambulance chaser • antitrust laws • appeal • arbitrary and ca

• armed and dangerous • as is • assumpsit • attorney • b.m.w. • bad debt • bait and switch • bankrupt • bankruptcy •bar •bar review course • basis • benc

vidence rule • big gun •bilious •billable hour •birdie •black acre • black letter law • blue book • bogart • bogie • boiler plate • bonus • book •boot •booty • bl

r • bust •busted • c.a.f.o. •calendar call • chain • child support •churning the file • circumstantial evidence •citation • class action • clearly • clients • clos

• coffee • comparative negligence • compensatorFy damages • consideration • constitutional law • contract • contributory negligence • contumacious •corpe

corpus delicti • counselor • creditor • cross examination • dead file • dead man's acts • deceit • deep pocket • de minimis non curat lex • demurrer • deposit

agatory clause • devil's dictionary • dictionary, law • directed verdict • disclosure • divorce • dormant commerce clause • dorr's Rebellion • double billing • dou

dy • due process • dying declaration • e.s.o.p. employee share ownership plan • eagle absence of malice • accessory • accomplice • acquit • act of god • act

vist judge • actus reus • administrative law • admiralty law • agent • albatross • alimony • alternative pleading • amnesty • ambulance chaser • antitrust law

l • arbitrary and capricious • armed and dangerous • as is • assumpsit • attorney • b m.w. • bad debt • bait and switch • bankrupt • bankruptcy •bar •bar rev

e • basis • bench • best evidence rule • big gun •bilious •billable hour •birdie •black acre • black letter law • blue book • bogart • bogie • boiler plate • bont

•boot •booty • bork •bribe • bust •busted • c a f o. •calendar call • chain • child support •churning the file • circumstantial evidence •citation • class actio

r • clients • closing costs • coffee • comparative negligence • compensatory damages • consideration • constitutional law • contract • contributory negligenc

macious •corporation • corpus delicti • counselor • creditor • cross examination • dead file • dead man's acts • deceit • deep pocket • de minimis non curat le

rer • deposition • derogatory clause • devil's dictionary • dictionary, law • directed verdict • disclosure • divorce • dormant commerce clause • dorr's Rebellio

e billing • double jeopardy • due process • dying declaration • e.s.o.p. employee share ownership plan • eagle • economic development program • ego • eig

dment •ejuration • entitlement • equal protection clause • equity • escheat •estate • estop • estoppel, equitable • ethics • evidence, laws of / rules of • excl

nce • exclusionary rule • exculpatory evidence rule • exhaustion of remedies • ex-wife/ex-husband • face time • fair • fair use doctrine • fairway • false arres

l judge • federalism • federal witness protection program • federalist society • fifth amendment • filibuster • first amendment • floating crap game • fourtee

dment • fourth amendment • force majeure • franking privilege •fraud • frivolous • fruit of the poisonous tree • fundamental right • garden • general denial • ge

• gift causa mortis • gift tax • gloss • good samaritan statues • got my papers! • great compromise • graft • gross • guarantee clause • guilt • h.a.p. • hab

s • habitability • habitability, warrantee of • hack • hand, Learned • harmless error • harvard law • hassle • hazardous • hazardous waste • headnote • hearsa

ARCHER, HUNTER, AND FISHER SPECIALISTS IN NATURAL RESOURCE DAMAGES

absence of malice. A phrase taken from *New York Times Co. v. Sullivan*, 376 U.S. 254 (1964), meaning that reporters can disseminate lies, half-truths, and wild accusations without incurring any liability for the harm they cause.

abuse of process. The use of legal process to achieve some illegitimate goal unrelated to the legitimate purpose of the process, such as using a subpoena to get a chance to ask out that really hot babe you haven't had the chance to chat up properly.

accessory. A removable hardtop and an infrared heads-up display—air conditioning, cruise control, power windows, power locks, and heated leather seats with power five-way adjustment are standard equipment on cars driven by self-respecting attorneys.

accomplice. Ambrose Bierce defined an accomplice as: "One associated with another in a crime, having guilty knowledge and complicity, as an attorney who defends a criminal, knowing him guilty. This view of the attorney's position in the matter has not hitherto commanded the assent of attorneys, no one having offered them a fee for assenting."[1] Seeing the truth of this statement, defense attorneys now instruct their

---

[1] Ambrose Bierce, *The Devil's Dictionary*, 1906

clients not to tell them anything about their involvement in a crime. This also avoids the inconvenience of working the truth into their case.

acquit. 1. To vote no confidence in a prosecutor. 2. A redneck resigning.

act of God. An archaic expression describing any natural disaster that caused a loss that could have been avoided but for the negligence of a wealthy American corporation.

action. It is ironic that attorneys should chose this word to designate the proceedings that form the core of their stock and trade. *Action* and *lawyer* are two words that nobody outside the legal profession—particularly clients—would associate with each other.

activist judge. A jurist who issues a decision within a year of hearing a case, motion, or appeal.

actus reus. "You can think about it, but *doonnnn't* do it."

administrative law. More due than process.

admiralty law. Whatever floats your boat...or sinks it.

agent. If you want something done right, do it yourself. Otherwise, keep your liability insurance premium paid on time.

aggravating circumstance. 1. Working in an office with "pods," "workstations," or "an open floor plan." 2. Having to compete for a promotion with the boss's child, cousin, nephew, or son/daughter/brother/sister-in-law. 3. Having to work for the boss's child, cousin, nephew, or son/daughter/brother/sister-in-law after (s)he gets the promotion.

alimony. 1. Severance pay for departing homemakers. 2. From each according to his philandering, to each according to her ire.

allodial title. Absolute title to real property free of any encumbrances or superior claims. It cannot be taken by operation of law for any reason. This form of title is rare in the United States, which perpetuated the tenurial system, in which title to property derives from the sovereign. Some self-proclaimed legal purists refuse to pay property tax on the grounds that the Treaty of Paris and state constitutions created allodial title to land in the United States at the end of the Revolutionary War. So far, courts have not stopped the law enforcement officers from throwing these kooks into the street after the tax sales of their property.

alternative dispute resolution. 1. An extra-judicial process in which parties present their position in a negotiation or conflict to a supposedly unbiased third party who attempts to settle the conflict by making each party equally unhappy with the outcome. 2. A way station on the road to litigation.

alternative pleading. Arguing in favor of two or more mutually exclusive or contradictory theories in one document. When lawyers do this, they consider themselves to be thorough. When doctors, teachers, engineers, or other professionals do it, lawyers consider it fodder for impeachment and malpractice claims.

ambulance chaser. A quaint expression referring to personal injury lawyers who pressed their business cards upon accident victims as soon as they arrived at the hospital. The practice has fallen out of favor because advertising in mass media allows sleazy tort lawyers to stay in their offices while attracting throngs of people eager to stick it to someone else.

amnesty. A selective retroactive recision of a penal statute for the benefit of particular offenders who it would be too inconvenient to prosecute or for a class of offenders who have good lobbyists.

answer. 1. A reply to a question in which the speaker attempts to avoid providing any information useful to the inquisitor. 2. A pleading responsive to a complaint in which the defendant attempts to avoid admitting anything useful to the plaintiff.

antitrust laws. Federal statutes that punish businesses for succeeding. In addition to the monetary disincentives to success, the antitrust laws allow the government to dismantle the offending business and create smaller, less profitable businesses.

appeal. A tactic by which litigation may be indefinitely prolonged by requesting a superior court to review the determinations of a lower court. *See remand.*

arbitrary and capricious. For a court to overturn the decision or action of an administrative agency, it must find that the decision or action was arbitrary and capricious. This standard demonstrates the low expectations we have of our government.

armed and dangerous. One of many phrases used in law that contains redundant or otherwise superfluous words thought to add a dramatic flare or solemnity to the proclamation. The net result is absurdity. Have you ever heard of someone being armed and harmless?

as is. "Whatever I'm selling to you is junk."

assigned counsel. An attorney assigned by a court to represent an indigent defendant. In return for their services to the benefit of society, the county or state pays the assigned counsel at a rate slightly lower than the wages earned by the courthouse janitors.

assumpsit. An archaic legal term that remains listed in law dictionaries because it sounds dirty but isn't.

attendant circumstances. An element of a crime external to the definition of the specific offense charged. For example, some jurisdictions require that prosecutors prove that the defendant is not a sympathetic character who had a bad break. After all, only all-around rotten jerks deserve to go to jail.

attorney. In the hierarchy of the legal profession, being called an attorney places one a notch above the lowest level, which is lawyer. *See also big gun, counselor, and warhorse.*

author. The creator of a work, particularly a writing, that has been rewritten by an editor, formatted, compiled, printed, and distributed by a publisher, and excoriated by critics.

authority, judicial. The opinion of someone who has a more impressive resumé than you do. Attorneys' pervasive use of judicial authority to support every mundane point of their arguments suggests the existence of a profession-wide inferiority complex that stifles original thought and prevents the application of common sense to any legal problem.

autoptic evidence. Seeing is believing.

7

autoptic proference. Bringing forth an exhibit in court to offer its admission into evidence. Preferably, this is done with the exhibit as close to the jury as possible prior to the request for admission and with an extended offer of proof so that the jury gets a good look at it no matter what.

BONES, HURT & AIKEN
SPECIALIZING IN:
PERSONAL INJURY
WORKERS' COMPENSATION
REPETITIVE MOTION
AND
WHIPLASH

bad debt. 1. *archaic*. Any debt. 2. *modern*. Any debt that you cannot pay off by making minimum payments for the rest of your life after taking out a consolidation loan and rolling it into a home equity line of credit for 135% of the value of your house, assuming your bank is the beneficiary of your life insurance policy.

bail. 1. To leave quickly. 2. What people tend to do after they post money with a court to secure their release from custody pending trial.

bait and switch. A sales technique so effective that it has been made illegal for retailers (but not for law firms). In the retail situation, the seller advertises an inexpensive item. The purchaser comes to the store only to find that the seller does not have the advertised item—but it does have a similar and more expensive item. In the law firm, the prospective client meets with a partner or partners during the initial consultation. After the client's check for the retainer has cleared, the law firm assigns a first-year associate to handle the case.

bankrupt. The state of being that you attain when the government sticks your creditors with the bill for your extravagant expenditures.

bankruptcy. 1. Legalized theft. (What else do you call taking money from someone and never giving it back?) 2. An adjective describing any of the institutions or procedures associated with government promotion of financially irresponsible behavior. 3. Proof that politicians have never read the works of John Locke, heard the parable of the Ant and the Grasshopper, or listened to the story of the Little Red Hen.

bar. 1. The lawyers collectively admitted to practice within a particular jurisdiction. 2. An examination used to separate those who are obsessed with law from those who merely want a good job. 3. A public house that serves alcoholic beverages. 4. The decisions of the Supreme Court are "entitled to just so much moral weight as would be the judgement of a majority of those congregated in any Washington barroom."[2]

bar review course. A series of classes taken by law school graduates in which they learn that they wasted three years and $100,000 on law school when they could have learned everything they needed to know to become a practicing lawyer in six weeks for less than $4,000.

basis. In tax and finance, the price paid to acquire property or a surrogate value for that price. This amount is used to calculate the gain that accrues to

---
[2] The *New York Tribune*, commenting on the *Dred Scott* decision

the property owner upon sale of the property. Gain equals sale price minus basis. The idea is to limit tax liability to the gain rather than the entire sale price. This seems fair. But gain is calculated using the present value of money without any adjustment for inflation. Consequently, government takes money that does not represent a gain in value. Not surprisingly, when it comes to calculating penalties and payments overdue to the I.R.S. and other agencies, the government employs sophisticated multi-variable computer programs that calculate the effects of inflation and adjust the amount due into current dollars.

Belli, Melvin Mouron (1907–1996). 1. An attorney who pioneered the use of demonstrative evidence. He also started the onslaught of the personal injury litigation we now face—earning himself the monikers "King of Torts" and "Melvin Bellicose," which must have been better than the nicknames he had while in grade school if anyone there knew about his middle name. 2. For law students who play bar trivia, Belli was a sometime actor who appeared as himself on television and in movies. He played the Gorgan in the painfully bad Star Trek episode "And the Children Shall Lead."

bench. To remove players from a game or games so that they must watch their teammates from the sidelines. This is the derivation of the designation of judges as *members of the bench*.

best evidence rule. A rule of evidence requiring that to prove the contents of a document, the original document must be offered into evidence—unless it is lost, destroyed, or legally unavailable. Technology is eroding this rule like a sand castle in the surf.

big gun. A powerhouse lawyer at the penultimate level of success, power, and respect in the legal profession. The mere mention of a big gun's name makes opposing attorneys sweat. Big guns are especially dangerous since they are still hungry for victory at any price, since they have not been at the top long enough to amass all the money and power that success at the highest echelons of law can provide.

bilious. Spiteful, bad-tempered, disputatious, and ill-natured—the essential characteristics of judges and senior partners.

billable hour. A period of time that contains 360 potential billable minutes. One hour billed in minimum increments of 1/10th of an hour allows for 60 one-minute tasks to be charged as 6 minutes of billable time each, or 360 minutes. Through double billing, a full 720 billable minutes are theoretically possible but not practically sustainable.

birdie. One stroke under par for a particular hole on a golf course.

Blackacre. The name used to identify real property in hypothetical law school fact patterns. This absurd holdover from feudal days when English lords named their estates illustrates the progressive nature of legal education. Rebellious professors sometimes name their imaginary estates Whiteacre or Greenacre.

Black, Hugo. Associate Justice of the United Sates Supreme Court from 1937 to 1971. Black was once involved with the KKK and was reputedly a religious bigot. Ironically, his religious intolerance may have caused him to take positions on the First Amendment that made him a favorite of many liberals, demonstrating that law—like politics—makes strange bedfellows.

black letter law. A term used to indicate positive law, particularly statutes. The term connotes the clear and binding nature of statutes. Judges often use the term to justify the rigid application of a law in a way that satisfies policy goals at the expense of manifest injustice to the individuals before the court.

blue book. This Harvard Law Review publication derives its name from the distinctive color of its cover—which is funny because Harvard's school color is crimson. Harvard touts it as the gold-standard reference for matters of style in the format of legal citations. That the manual for concisely identifying references requires a book an inch thick with minuscule typefaces should serve as a warning to all would-be lawyers that they are entering a profession controlled by anal-retentive detail freaks who exalt form over substance.

B.M.W. Bavarian Motor Works, or any of a variety of over-priced status symbols produced by that company and leased to young attorneys who cannot afford them.

bogart. To acquire by stealth that which your friend held in his possession and to which neither of you held a practically enforceable right of ownership. E.g., "Don't bogart my seat at the bar while I'm in the men's room," or "Hey! Who bogartted the last beer?"

bogie. One stoke over par for a particular hole of a golf course. A double bogie is two strokes over par and so forth.

boilerplate. Within a legal document, a passage or section that the drafter has used repeatedly in similar documents without change. This allows the lawyer to charge a large fee for doing nothing.

bonus. 1. Money paid to associates based on performance exceeding expectations. 2. Alms for the secure.

book. 1. *Slang.* To flee or leave quickly. 2. What police do to perpetrators who fail to do number 1.

boot. 1. Money or property added to a transaction to create an equal exchange. For example, your ex-spouse gives you years of misery. You give him or her $5,000 a month, half your 401(k), and the house to boot. 2. Slang for vomit, which is what you do in the courthouse bathroom when you realize that the judge has just awarded your ex-spouse $5,000 a month, half of your 401(k), and the house to boot.

booty. That which people pursue with greatest passion. *Archaic:* Property captured in war, privateering, or piracy. *Modern:* A well-shaped posterior accentuated by a narrow waist and tight-fitting clothes.

bork. To deny confirmation of a qualified judicial nominee for purely political reasons. This was first done to Roger B. Taney when Daniel Webster prevented Taney's confirmation as Andrew Jackson's Secretary of the Treasury and again defeated his nomination as Associate Justice of the United States

Supreme Court. But "Taneyed" doesn't sound as nasty as "Borked," so it never caught on.

bribe. To offer something of value to a public official to induce the official to use the power of his or her position to one's own benefit. However, as long as the payer does not specify the desired recompense until after the recipient cashes the check, the payment is known as a campaign contribution.

bullshit. Bullshit includes hyperbole, obfuscation, and any other form of deceptive communication. This describes most of what lawyers produce, and it is the reason most people rank lawyers below politicians, prostitutes, and used car dealers on their lists of society's parasites.

bust. The upper portion of the female torso that young female professionals flaunt to the greatest extent possible but which male attorneys are not allowed to glance at, comment on, or notice in any way without risking career-ending charges of sexual harassment.

busted. To be caught in an illegal or illicit act, such as glancing at the barely contained upper torso of a female coworker.

17

d debt • bait and switch • bankrupt • bankruptcy •bar •bar review course • basis • bench • best evidence rule • big gun •bilious •billable hour •birdie •black

ack letter law • blue book • bogart • bogie • boiler plate • bonus • book •boot •booty • bork •bribe • bust •busted • c.a.f.o. •calendar call • chain • child s

uming the file • circumstantial evidence •citation • class action • clearly • clients • closing costs • coffee • comparative negligence • compensatory dama

sideration • constitutional law • contract • contributory negligence • contumacious •corporation • corpus delicti • counselor • creditor • cross examination • dea

ad man's acts • deceit • deep pocket • de minimis non curat lex • demurrer • deposition • derogatory clause • devil's dictionary • dictionary, law • directed v

sclosure • divorce • dormant commerce clause • dorr's Rebellion • double billing • double jeopardy • due process • dying declaration • e.s.o.p. employee share o

plan • eagle • economic development program • ego • eighth amendment •ejuration • entitlement • equal protection clause • equity • escheat •estate • es

ppel, equitable • ethics • evidence, laws of / rules of • excited utterance • exclusionary rule • exculpatory evidence rule • exhaustion of remedies • ex-wi

band • face time • fair • fair use doctrine • fairway • false arrest • federal judge • federalism • federalism • federal witness protection program • federalist s

th amendment • fifteenth amendment • filibuster • first amendment • floating crap game • fourteenth amendment • fourth amendment • force majeure • fr

lege •fraud • frivolous • fruit of the poisonous tree • fundamental right • garden • general denial • gerrymander • gift causa mortis • gift tax • gloss • good s

statues • got my papers! • great compromise • graft • gross • guarantee clause • guilt • h.a.p. • habeas corpus • habitability • habitability, warrantee of • l

l, Learned • harmless error • harvard law • hassle • hazardous • hazardous waste • headnote • hearsay • heirloom • hereinabove, hereinafter, heretofore • he

said • homicide • hornbook • hose • hundred weight • hung jury • ill fame • immoral • impediment to marriage • import-export clause • imputed negligence • im

corporation by reference • income • inchoate • indemnity • indigent • inevitable discovery rule • infancy • internal Revenue code • internal Revenue service •

ual property • interstate commerce • ipso facto • irrelevant • jack • jeopardy • judicial review • jump • jail • jailhouse lawyer • joint and several liability • journ

• judge • judgment • judgment not withstanding the verdict • jurisprudence • jury • jury instructions • jury wheel • just compensation • justice • justification • l

uver-cellars act • kentucky rule • kick • kickback • kilo • kiting • kleptomania • knock and announce • know • know-it-all • known-heirs • laches, estoppel by •

ract • lapse in judgement • law • law of the case • law review • lawyer's trust account • lead counsel • legislative intent • liability • libel • link • liquidated dar

igation • loaded • long-arm jurisdiction • lose • maintenance • malice aforethought • malicious prosecution • malpractice insurance • manual labor • making a

arriage • marrone • mason • matlock, ben • maundering • mcnaughton Rule • mendacity • mens rea • merely • minnesota twins, the • monopoly • mortgage

• multi-state • navigable waters • negligence • new york • new york lawyers • ninth amendment • no-knock warrant • not-for-profit corporation • nutshell •

rn • objection • obscenity • offer • old bailey • oligarchy • originalist • paternity • paternity test • palimony • penultimate • perspicuity • pike test • plea ba

essey v. ferguson • potter, stewart • poverty law • pornography • prevarication • product liability • professional responsibility • prior inconsistent statement •

aint • prolix • public interest law • public interest lawyer • punitive damages • quantum meruit • quash • quarter section • question presented • quid pro quo •

n deed • rainmaker • rational basis test • rejection • remand • residuum • residuum rule • res ipsa loquitor • res judicata • respondent superior • responsible •

• rule against perpetuities • screw • screw-the-pooch • second amendment • sentence • separation of powers • settlement • seventh amendment • sinking f

eenth amendment • sixth amendment • slander • solicitation • spendthrift • stare decisis • stages of marriage • statute • statutes of frauds • street lawyer •

struction • strict scrutiny • sub rosa • substantive due process • sudden heat of passion • summer associate • taylor law • take it upstairs • taxation • tenth a

at • think-they-know-it-all • third amendment • tickle • title insurance • tort • to wit • traduce • trespass • trust • ultimate • unambiguous • unconstitutional • ur

mercial code • unique • united states supreme court • unjust enrichment • usury • usufruct • vagrant • verified pleading • very • waiver • warhorse • war

ess • warranty, implied • warranty period • ways-and-means • webster, daniel • west publishing • whole-life insurance • wirt, william • withholding • yield •

kel • zealous representation • zone of interest test • zoning • absence of malice • accessory • accomplice • acquit • act of god • action • activist judge • actu

ministrative law • admiralty law • agent • albatross • alimony • alternative pleading • amnesty • ambulance chaser • antitrust laws • appeal • arbitrary and

s • armed and dangerous • as is • assumpsit • attorney • b.m.w • bad debt • bait and switch • bankrupt • bankruptcy •bar •bar review course • basis • be

, evidence rule • big gun •bilious •billable hour •birdie •black acre • black letter law • blue book • bogart • bogie • boiler plate • bonus • book •boot •booty •

he • bust •busted • c.a.f.o. •calendar call • chain • child support •churning the file • circumstantial evidence •citation • class action • clearly • clients • c

s • coffee • comparative negligence • compensatory damages • consideration • constitutional law • contract • contributory negligence • contumacious •co

• corpus delicti • counselor • creditor • cross examination • dead file • dead man's acts • deceit • deep pocket • de minimis non curat lex • demurrer • depo

rogatory clause • devil's dictionary • dictionary, law • directed verdict • disclosure • divorce • dormant commerce clause • dorr's Rebellion • double billing • d

ardy • due process • dying declaration • e.s.o.p. employee share ownership plan • eagle absence of malice • accessory • accomplice • acquit • act of god •

tivist judge • actus reus • administrative law • admiralty law • agent • albatross • alimony • alternative pleading • amnesty • ambulance chaser • antitrust la

eal • arbitrary and capricious • armed and dangerous • as is • assumpsit • attorney • b.m.w • bad debt • bait and switch • bankrupt • bankruptcy •bar •bar r

rse • basis • bench • best evidence rule • big gun •bilious •billable hour •birdie •black acre • black letter law • blue book • bogart • bogie • boiler plate • bo

• boot •booty • bork •bribe • bust •busted • c.a.f.o. •calendar call • chain • child support •churning the file • circumstantial evidence •citation • class ac

rly • clients • closing costs • coffee • comparative negligence • compensatory damages • consideration • constitutional law • contract • contributory neglige

tumacious •corporation • corpus delicti • counselor • creditor • cross examination • dead file • dead man's acts • deceit • deep pocket • de minimis non curat

urrer • deposition • derogatory clause • devil's dictionary • dictionary, law • directed verdict • disclosure • divorce • dormant commerce clause • dorr's Rebel

ble billing • double jeopardy • due process • dying declaration • e.s.o.p. employee share ownership plan • eagle • economic development program • ego • e

ndment • ejuration • entitlement • equal protection clause • equity • escheat •estate • estop • estoppel, equitable • ethics • evidence, laws of / rules of • e

rance • exclusionary rule • exculpatory evidence rule • exhaustion of remedies • ex-wife/ex-husband • face time • fair • fair use doctrine • fairway • false ar

eral judge • federalism • federal witness protection program • federalist society • fifth amendment • filibuster • first amendment • floating crap game • fourt

ndment • fourth amendment • force majeure • franking privilege •fraud • frivolous • fruit of the poisonous tree • fundamental right • garden • general denial •

der • gift causa mortis • gift tax • gloss • good samaritan statues • got my papers! • great compromise • graft • gross • guarantee clause • guilt • h.a.p. • h

us • habitability • habitability, warrantee of • hack • hand, Learned • harmless error • harvard law • hassle • hazardous • hazardous waste • headnote • heat

aaaa • hereinabove, hereinafter, heretofore • he said, she said • homicide • hornbook • hose • hundred weight • hung jury • ill fame • immoral • impedin

CAGE AND CAINE
ATTORNEYS AT LAW
CRIMINAL DEFENSE
AND
PRISONERS' RIGHTS

C.A.F.O. Concentrated Animal Feeding Operation. A supermax prison for livestock.

calendar call. Bringing in the sleaze.

Campbell, John A. Associate Justice of the United States Supreme Court from 1853 to 1861. Although from Alabama, he advocated a voluntary end to slavery and disagreed with the reasoning in Chief Justice Taney's *Dred Scott* opinion. He opposed secession; however, he returned to Alabama when it joined the Confederacy, probably just to spite Jefferson Davis and the South. Although the Confederate Constitution called for a judicial branch of government, the Confederacy never constituted one because they couldn't figure out how to prevent Campbell from using it to be a pain in their ass.

cash basis accounting. A method of handling monetary or business transactions that minimizes paperwork and reduces the gross taxable income of the payee. The method is highly efficient and easy to learn, making it popular with small businesspeople and service personnel who process large numbers of small transactions.

Celotex v. Catrett, **477 U.S. 317 (1986).** A case that decided a party may win a summary judgment motion without submitting any cognizable evidence, but the party opposing the motion must "lay bare its proof" to avoid losing. So, a party with the burden of proof can, theoretically, win without producing any admissible evidence.

chain. A linear measurement, commonly used in descriptions of real property, equaling four rods. This explains why men have been lying about the size of rods for time immemorial.

child support. A law of gravity.

churning the file. Stealing from a client by billing for unnecessary activities. The theft is almost never prosecuted because one man's "pointless waste of time" is another man's "diligent attention to detail."

cigar. Chopped tobacco rolled in a tobacco leaf to form a tightly packed cylinder. The cigar is utilized by igniting one end so that the tobacco slowly smolders, emitting an acrid smell that repels a host of pests, including spouses, paramours, clients, secretaries, and other lawyers.

circumstantial evidence. A presentation of facts from which the existence of additional facts or circumstances may be inferred. For example, if the ground is bare when one goes to bed and it is covered with snow when one awakes, one may reasonably infer that the snowplow has created a massive snowbank blocking the end of one's driveway.

citation. A reference to legal authority signified by long strings of random words, numbers, and symbols inserted into the text of a document to interrupt the reader's attention to the actual argument.

class action. A procedure for turning insignificant individual losses into massive contingency fees for trial lawyers.

clearly. A favorite word of lawyers, it means nothing and should never be used. If a matter is self-evident, calling it so will not add to its persuasive force. If a matter is not clear, then saying that it is will not make it so. *See merely.*

clients. Persons for whom lawyers convert fears and problems into legal fees and judgments.

closing costs. A litany of fees paid by the buyer at a real estate closing, most of which are imposed by the lender to cover expenses—as if they haven't already built those costs into the interest rates that they charge and from which they will reap pure profit with minimal effort for 15 to 40 years.

coffee. A bitter potion consumed in large quantities to alter one's consciousness before meditative periods of studying the holy case reports and sacred statues. Law students often overdose in their quest for transcendental moments of complete enlightenment before facing the ritual sacrifice of the blue book.

colorable argument. Any dubious claim that has the merest thread of connection with a possible application of relevant law to a potentially plausible fact. Normal people call this bullshit. *See zealous representation.*

comparative negligence. A doctrine that allows even the foolish and careless access to the deep pockets of defendants' insurance companies. *See contributory negligence.*

compensatory damages. A monetary award in an amount intended to "make a plaintiff whole" by replacing the money lost to the plaintiff due to the actions of the defendant, and which—after deduction of fees, costs, the value of time, and incidental expenses—leaves the plaintiff with even less than he had before the suit. *See punitive damages.*

Comprehensive Environmental Response Compensation and Liability Act & Superfund Amendment and Reauthorization Act (C.E.R.C.L.A. & S.A.R.A.). "You clean it up and we'll tell you when you're done."

consideration. To normal people, this means thoughtfulness. To lawyers, it means something subjectively valuable, especially money.

constitution. A written document setting forth fundamental laws that politicians and bureaucrats spend their time attempting to circumvent—for the good of the people, of course.

constitutional law. What five justices of the United States Supreme Court think on any given day.

contract. An agreement enforceable-at-law that serves as a starting point for future negotiations.

contributory negligence. A draconian doctrine that prohibits people who injure themselves through their own negligence from blaming others for the injury and making them pay.

contumacious. Persistently insubordinate or contemptuous of authority. Business owners and public interest lawyers—people who have the natural affinity of a cobra and a mongoose—share this trait.

24

corporation. An imaginary friend who takes the blame for everything you do wrong.

corpus delicti. The body against which a crime has been committed. Examples include, for different reasons, Pamela Anderson and Randall "Tex" Cobb.

counselor. Being called counselor denotes respect and places one above the level of attorney and below the lofty status of big gun in the hierarchy of the legal profession. However, *counselor* is one of the few words in English that derives its meaning as much from tone as enunciation. If the speaker exaggerates the syllables and lengthens the pronunciation, *counselor* becomes a word of derision. When pronounced in this way, it means that you have done or said something so ludicrous that the speaker feels compelled to remind you that you attended law school and should have learned something there.

creditor. An entity with an excess of money that increases its wealth and simultaneously ensures that other people remain impoverished by loaning them money to buy items they cannot afford at an ultimate cost far exceeding the value of the item purchased.

cross-examination. The interrogation of a witness who testified on behalf of an opposing party during an adversarial proceeding. Clients universally expect cross-examination to be a blistering attack that leaves the opposing witnesses—especially the opposing party—looking like a liar, a moron, or preferably both. Many lawyers blame television and movies—*Law and Order, A Few Good Men*, etc.—for their clients' expectations of cross-examination. Clients really want vicious cross-examinations because they don't acknowledge the existence of the other party's perspective, they don't want the judge to hear the other side of the case, and they want to beat the hell out of the opposing party and shut him up. Because they can't do that in court, they hope that cross-examination will inflict as much misery and humiliation as possible.

DeBeers and Schotz, P.L.L.C.
D.U.I.s
Liquor Licenses
Dramshop Liability

Dartmouth v. Woodward, 17 U.S. (4 Wheat.) 518 (1819). This is known as the Dartmouth College case. It was the last hurrah for Chief Justice John Marshall and the contract clause of the United States Constitution.

Daubert v. Merrill Dow Pharmaceuticals, 509 U.S. 579 (1993). Made "She Blinded Me With Science" the theme of the federal district courts.

dead file. A case or transaction from which no more fees can be extracted.

dead man's acts. In a rare act of common sense, legislatures in most states have enacted laws that prohibit testimony from those who have passed beyond the veil. The universal condemnation of this policy by law professors and elite practitioners confirms its wisdom. *Refer to Weinstein's Evidence at 601-20-21 (1985).*

deceit. 1. An artifice or contrivance used to trick another. 2. An essential element of successful tort and criminal defense litigation. 3. Yet another reason for people to rank lawyers below used car salesmen, politicians, and prostitutes.

deep pocket. A party sued because of its ability to pay astronomical judgments, particularly where the party did not directly cause the plaintiff's injury. *See also respondent superior.*

default. A failure to respond to a pleading or appear in court, resulting in an adverse decision. The term derives from the litany of excuses that flow from the defaulting parties once they learn of the consequences of their omission to act. E.g., "It's d'fault of my lawyer," "It's d'fault of the mail," "It's d'fault of my medication," and so on and so on.

delay. One of the four cornerstones of the legal system. *See also deceit, due process, and billable hours.*

de minimis non curat lex. The law does not concern itself with small things. Neither will you if you want to make money.

demurrer. A responsive pleading stating "so what."

deposition. A pretrial oral interrogation of a person who has knowledge or evidence relevant to litigation. Most attorneys seem incapable of distinguishing this from cross-examination. Ironically, attorneys capable of conducting good cross-examinations are the ones who know enough to avoid a cross-examination of a witness during a deposition. Also called *examination before trial.*

derogatory clause. A secret phrase, sentence, code, or symbol known only to the testator and his lawyer, coupled with a provision that no future will or codicil executed by the testator is valid unless it also contains the secret wording or symbol. This protects the testator against forgery and extortion. Unfortunately, your network administrator or Internet service provider will not email your derogatory clause to you if you forget it.

Devil's Dictionary, The. A compilation of scathing aphorisms and observations by American satirist Ambrose Bierce. First published one hundred years ago, the copyright has expired, making the book a "timeless classic" promoted by several publishers who will not have to pay royalties.

dictionary, law. A bloated tome filled with ostensibly important legal terms of art that are supported by outdated or irrelevant citations. After being purchased by insecure first-year law students, the main purpose of these weighty volumes is to bend cheap book-shelves. Lawyers rarely consult a law dictionary because any definition they need to know will come from a reported case or statute. In days gone by, the law dictionary occasionally provided a befuddled lawyer with a place to start his or her research. Electronic research has since made law dictionaries superfluous.

diesel therapy. Prosecutors and penal officials are able to effectively upgrade a prisoner's sentence from minimum security to maximum security—and screw with his head—by arranging pretexts for the inmate to be transported to locations distant from the prison to which he was initially assigned. While en route, the inmate is kept in higher security facilities, kept out of touch with his family, and kept as disconcerted as possible.

directed verdict. A declaration by the court that the plaintiff's case was a colossal waste of time and money.

disclosure. The lawyer's version of a treasure hunt, played primarily with paper. This game is more exciting than a normal treasure hunt in two ways. First, the players must create their own list of items that they need to find in order to win. Second, rules allow offensive play—finding the items one must have to win—and defensive play—preventing your opponent from obtaining the items they need. Also called *discovery*.

divorce. The dissolution of the legal relationship of marriage. People mistakenly expect this to terminate their personal relationship. In practice, divorce merely increases the number of things the parties have to fight about.

dormant commerce clause. Presto chango! Through the magic of legal mumbo jumbo, the affirmative power of Congress over interstate commerce has become an avenue by which federal courts get to review the political correctness of any state law that affects commerce. Whether a law will affect interstate commerce is determined by asking, "What would happen if everyone did that at the same time?"

Dorr's Rebellion. A revolt against the oppressive government existing in post-colonial Rhode Island. This caused two governments to exist within that state for a time and resulted in the Supreme Court excising the Guarantee Clause from the United States Constitution.

double billing. Two clients can occupy the same lawyer at the same time.

double jeopardy. Popular term for Fifth Amendment provision stating " . . . nor shall any person be subject for the same offense to be twice put in jeopardy . . ."

Which, after interpretations by the Supreme Court, means a person may be prosecuted at most three times for the same offense—once in a state criminal court, once in federal criminal proceedings, and if that goes badly, once in federal court for violating someone's civil rights. *Refer to Moore v. Illinois, 55 U.S. (14 How.) 13 (1852).*

Dred Scott case (*Scott v. Sandford*, 60 U.S. 393 (1857)). A towering example of the benefits of a powerful and activist judiciary. The United States Supreme Court ignored judicial convention and contrived reasons to resolve the festering political disputes regarding limitations on the westward expansion of slavery by fiat. Fortunately, the Court is subject to checks and balances. Four years of Civil War and three Constitutional amendments lessened the influence of this precedent until the Court regrouped and gave us *Plessy v. Ferguson.*

dubious. An adjective used to describe every potentially valid argument or factual assertion made by an opponent. Any truly damaging statements made by an opponent are "highly dubious." The "highly" part of the phrase is important because without that, you can't be sure your reader will realize that you think your opponent is a deceptive jerk.

due process. The application of lawfully established procedures to maximize the time and expense needed for government to make the simplest decision, and whenever possible, prevent government from taking any action whatsoever.

dying declaration. Dying declarations are admissible despite being hearsay. The rationale begins with the obvious fact that the declarant is unavailable to testify. Courts presume that someone who knows he is about to die would not waste his last gasp and would not want to meet his maker with the stain of a lie on his soul. Many modern legal thinkers reject this reasoning on the grounds that if someone does make their dying statement a lie, it will be a whopper.

EVAN, STEVEN, AND GLAD, P.L.L.C.
ASSISTING BUSINESSES WITH
CONTRACTS
REMEDIES
AND THE
UNIFORM COMMERCIAL CODE

economic development program. A bureaucracy through which elected officials provide jobs or taxpayers' money to their friends and contributors, and through which government "invests" taxpayers' money in harebrained schemes that no private investor or bank will support.

ego. A portion of the lawyer's makeup that has a tendency toward uncontrollable swelling. This can cause an inability to function normally in public. Mild cases can be cured by a shocking blow. If left untreated, the ego has a tendency to harden and become invulnerable. Removal of hardened egos causes severe trauma and should therefore be left to enemies who will really enjoy watching the victim suffer.

Eighth Amendment. This Amendment of the United States Constitution prohibits cruel and unusual punishment. As modern jurists focus only on the word "cruel" in this provision, and because all punishments involve some measure of cruelty, the constitutionality of the entire penal system is currently in doubt.

ejuration. 1. The only method by which a member of a state legislature or the United States Congress leaves office while alive. 2. Something most politicians would do if they placed the nation's interests above their own.

entitlement. Any of a number of government programs through which politicians use tax dollars to buy votes.

Equal Protection Clause. A clause of the Fourteenth Amendment of the United States Constitution that was effectively quashed by the nineteenth-century Supreme Court. This was later deemed a mistake. Because the Court is incapable of admitting errors, the justices decided to misconstrue the Due Process Clause to compensate for the prior bad decisions regarding the Equal Protection Clause.

equity, court of. Historically, separate courts existed for actions at law for money damages and actions in equity for injunctive relief. The distinction lost practical relevance in modern times, the object of all litigation being to screw the opposing party one way or another.

Erie Railroad v. Tompkins, **304 U.S. 64 (1938).** In 1789, Congress enacted the Federal Judiciary Act. Section 34 of the Act stated that "the laws of the several states shall be considered the rules of decision in trials at common law," unless they conflicted with federal law. In a herculean feat of intellectual abstraction, the Supreme Court determined that state court decisions were not law, and therefore federal courts were unfettered by the common law of the states. See *Swift v. Tyson,* 41 U.S. (16 Pet.) 1 (1842). The Supreme Court overruled *Swift* in *Erie* because Justice Brandies noticed the word "law" in "common law."

escheat. The transfer of property to the state pursuant to laws (enacted by the same state government) that make the government a potential beneficiary of every estate.

E.S.O.P. Employee Share Ownership Plan (or Employees Screwed On Purpose). An incentive system in which a corporation pays a portion of employees' salaries with stock in the employing company. This saves the corporation from spending cash because it can always issue more stock. It also gives corporate officers and directors the satisfaction of knowing that in addition to running a company into the ground and liquidating its assets, they can ruin the lives of innumerable hardworking people in the process.

estate. All wealth—property real and personal—owned by a person, ownership of which survives death long enough for the government to confiscate most of it.

estop. To prevent a party from engaging in an otherwise lawful activity because "it's just not fair!"

estoppel, equitable. A remedy imposed by courts of equity to ensure victory for the party that the judge favors.

ethics. *See professional responsibility.*

evidence, laws of / rules of. A complex system of legal gasconade including thousands of pages dealing with hundreds of cases and statutes, all of which ultimately boil down to allowing admission of evidence if it is reliable and relevant.

excited utterance. A statement provoked by a startling or shocking event. In the law of evidence, excited utterances are an exception to the prohibition against hearsay testimony. Some commentators question this exception to the hearsay rule on grounds that true excited utterances consist almost entirely of screams and expletives.

exclusionary rule. A doctrine created by the United States Supreme Court to punish society for the transgressions of the police.

exculpatory evidence rule. A prosecutor must help those who can't help themselves.

exhaustion of remedies. A doctrine that requires people who wish to challenge a decision or action of an administrative agency to fully pursue all avenues of redress offered by that agency before the judiciary will entertain the case. This reduces the case load of courts because most people exhaust their funds before exhausting the bureaucracy.

extenuating circumstance. Conditions that mitigate the seriousness of a wrongful or criminal act and may result in lenient treatment. Care must be taken when presenting extenuating circumstances because the evaluation of what constitutes an extenuating circumstance is subjective. To you, the fact that "that babe had a killer bod" might seem to be an extenuating circumstance when you stop to stare. To the judge, jury, and executioner—your spouse—this constitutes an aggravating circumstance that justifies cruel and unusual punishment.

extraordinary gain or loss. For most people, gains are more extraordinary than losses.

ex-wife/ex-husband. The marital status of lawyers who spent eighty hours per week entombed in their firm's law library in a fanatical quest to become a partner.

FIRST, DOWNS, PITCHER, AND HOMER, P.C.
COMPLETE REPRESENTATION FOR
ATHLETES

face time. Time spent by an unimportant or unknown person (such as a young lawyer) in the presence of an important individual (such as a law partner, elected official, or wealthy client) so that the more important person will remember the shlep when it comes time to bestow favors, promotions, assignments, political appointments, and other matters of value.

fair. 1. The winning party's description of a judgment or decision. 2. A place to get your face painted and ride a Ferris wheel.

fair use doctrine. An easement authorizing public access to intellectual property. The practical effect is that the copyright holder watches her supposed monopoly over her work disappear like a loaf of bread being attacked by a flock of ducks.

fairway. An open stretch of well-mown grass that provides time to collect your thoughts between the opening of a discussion at the tee and its conclusion at the green.

false arrest. A misapprehension.

federalism. A style of government involving two or more sovereignties exerting control over one set of people, as in the United States. The founding fathers inexplicably believed that one government regulating the people would be a threat to freedom, but *two* governments regulating individual behavior would secure individual liberty.

federalism, cooperative. Congress conditions expenditure of federal funds upon the states' implementation of federal policies that are outside the scope of the powers delegated to the federal government. For example, the Congress might decide that homosexual marriage should be legal. It cannot force states to legalize same-sex marriage, but it can refuse to spend money in states that do not recognize same-sex marriage. When the states capitulate, they are deemed cooperative.

Federalist Society. A group of extremist fringe radical kooks who espouse the bigoted ideology that "[it] is the province and duty of the judiciary to say what the law is, not what it should be."

federal judge. A politician whose term expires when (s)he does.

federal witness protection program. A Ponzi scheme in which criminals avoid their just punishments by offering evidence against more successful criminals who, in turn, offer to give evidence against still more successful criminals. The only criminal who

43

receives unmitigated punishment is the one who has nobody more villainous than himself to betray. However, the pace of our judicial system ensures that by the time someone rolls over on the boss of bosses, five days in jail for a speeding ticket would amount to a life sentence.

fertile octogenarian. This is a hypothetical fact pattern used by law professors to illustrate the absurdity of strict application of the rule against perpetuities. The example supposes that an elderly person, usually a woman, leaves her estate to "each of my children upon their 25th birthday." The gift fails because strictly applying the rule, the woman could have a child at 89 years of age and die at 90, and more than twenty-one years would pass before the property vested in the youngest child. The willingness of fertility clinics to use technology to impregnate anything with a pulse has made the fertile octogenarian less hypothetical, but no less absurd. Also, strictly applied, every gift of real property now fails under the rule against perpetuities because sperm, eggs, and even fertilized eggs can be stored indefinitely and implanted long after the death of anyone who happened to be alive at the time of the gift.

Fifteenth Amendment. The Amendment to the United States Constitution that granted African-Americans the right to vote from its ratification on February 3, 1870, until its "interpretation" by the Supreme Court in *James v. Bowman,* 190 U.S. 127 (1903).

Fifth Amendment. Under the progressive applications of the United States Constitution, this portion of the Bill of Rights provides an ever-widening cloak of protection for the personal liberty of criminals and a rapidly shrinking veil around the ownership of property.

file. 1. To place documents in a storage system organized in a manner that allows their rapid retrieval by the single person in the office who understands the system. Anyone else looking for a document after it has been filed will probably find the remains of Amelia Earhart's last plane before laying hands on the papers they want. 2. A collection of documents that, when last seen, was carefully organized in one place and which, when needed, becomes a morass of random data that defies all efforts of coordination.

filibuster. Formerly, this was an indefinitely long oration in a legislative chamber, particularly the United States Senate, meant to prevent legislative action. In modern times, it means counting noses to determine if the side favoring a measure has the required number of votes to halt the debate. This saves these important hardworking public servants the trouble of actually having to makes speeches or hold the floor during the debate. The result is that any slightly controversial measure is "filibustered" because other than spending other people's money, doing nothing is what politicians do best.

First Amendment. The Amendment of the United States Constitution that establishes atheism as the national belief system, (U.S. Const. Amd 1, cl. 1) guarantees the unrestricted distribution of pornography (U.S. Const. Amd. 1 cl. 2; *Roth v. United States,* 354 U.S. 476 (1957)), and authorizes Congress to prohibit people from disseminating opinions and information regarding political issues and candidates for public office (*McConnell v. Federal Election Commission,* 540 U.S. 93 (2003)).

floating crap game. An illegal or illicit game of chance played with dice that takes place at randomly changing locations to avoid detection by law enforcement. (Tonight we'll be behind Phil's Place on Chestnut Street.)

force majeure. An archaic doctrine pursuant to which a party is excused from liability because an intervening act of God prevented the party from meeting his obligation. (However, because the First

Amendment prohibits government from sanctioning the existence of a deity, force majeure clauses that use the phrase "act of God" are void *ab abnitio*.) When it comes down to it, a reasonable person expects to encounter a war, riot, strike, or natural disaster, and should have contingency plans.

Fourteenth Amendment. The Amendment of the United States Constitution that vested the federal judiciary with legislative powers and the authority to veto state laws.

Fourth Amendment. In December 1791, this addition to the United States Constitution prohibited officers of the federal government from searching homes and seizing papers and effects without a descriptive warrant based on probable cause to believe evidence of a crime would be discovered. Today, it allows the government to monitor cell-phone conversations and email messages but prohibits law makers from regulating birth control.

Francis v. Resweber, 329 U.S. 459 (1947). If at first the execution fails, fry, fry again.

franking privilege. The right of members of Congress to send campaign advertisements through the mail at taxpayers' expense.

fraud. 1. An intentional misrepresentation intended to induce another to act to the benefit of the perpetrator of the lie. 2. A person who perpetrates a complex lie or misrepresents his identity or intentions, as in a politician or trial lawyer.

frivolous. To most people, something frivolous involves pointless fun, as in frivolity. To lawyers, something is frivolous if it is devoid of substance or utterly without merit. For example, we have frivolous arguments, frivolous lawsuits, and so on. So, either lawyers are sadists who think that making people miserable is a light hobby, or we have a poor grasp of the language. Or both.

fruit of the poisonous tree. One little mistake and the prosecution's whole case unravels like a cheap sweater.

Frye v. United States, **293 F. 1013 (D.C. Cir. 1923).** With amazing insight, the Supreme Court coined the phrase "twilight zone" in relation to science fiction a year before Rod Serling was born. In doing so, it created the "general acceptance" test for the admission of scientific evidence. This standard endured for seven decades, until the best legal minds in the country wrote it out of the Federal Rules of Evidence and left judges on their own to decide whether some crackpot theory is bullshit or a cutting-edge discovery.

fundamental right. An individual liberty considered essential to the existence of a free society such that the government may only impede the exercise thereof if five of nine politically connected Ivy League alumni approve.

ad debt • bait and switch • bankrupt • bankruptcy •bar •bar review course • basis • bench • best evidence rule • big gun •bilious •billable hour •birdie •bla
ack letter law • blue book • bogart • bogie • boiler plate • bonus • book •boot •booty • bork •bribe • bust •busted • c.a.f.o. •calendar call • chain • child s
urning the file • circumstantial evidence •citation • class action • clearly • clients • closing costs • coffee • comparative negligence • compensatory dama
sideration • constitutional law • contract •contributory negligence • contumacious •corporation • corpus delicti • counselor • creditor • cross examination • de
ad man's acts • deceit • deep pocket • de minimis non curat lex • demurrer • deposition • derogatory clause • devil's dictionary • dictionary, law • directed
sclosure • divorce • dormant commerce clause • dorr's Rebellion • double billing • double jeopardy • due process • dying declaration • e.s.o.p. employee share o
plan • eagle • economic development program • ego • eighth amendment •ejuration • entitlement • equal protection clause • equity • escheat •estate • e
oppel, equitable • ethics • evidence, laws of / rules of • excited utterance • exclusionary rule • exculpatory evidence rule • exhaustion of remedies • ex-w
band • face time • fair • fair use doctrine • fairway • false arrest • federal judge • federalism • federalism • federal witness protection program • federalist s
th amendment • fifteenth amendment • filibuster • first amendment • floating crap game • fourteenth amendment • fourth amendment • force majeure • fra
ilege •fraud • frivolous • fruit of the poisonous tree • fundamental right • garden • general denial • gerrymander • gift causa mortis • gift tax • gloss • good s
statues • got my papers! • great compromise • graft • gross • guarantee clause • guilt • h.a.p. • habeas corpus • habitability • habitability, warrantee of • ll
d. Learned • harmless error • harvard law • hassle • hazardous • hazardous waste • headnote • hearsay • heirloom • hereinabove, hereinafter, heretofore • he
said • homicide • hornbook • hose • hundred weight • hung jury • ill fame • immoral • impediment to marriage • import-export clause • imputed negligence • in
corporation by reference • income • inchoate • indemnity • indigent • inevitable discovery rule • infancy • internal Revenue code • internal Revenue service •
ual property • interstate commerce • ipso facto • irrelevant • jack • jeopardy • judicial review • jump • jail • jailhouse lawyer • joint and several liability • jour
ilege • judgment • judgment not withstanding the verdict • jurisprudence • jury • jury instructions • jury wheel • just compensation • justice • justification •
huver-cellars act • kentucky rule • kick • kickback • kilo • kiting • kleptomania • knock and announce • know • know-it-all • known-heirs • laches, estoppel by
tract • lapse in judgement • law • law of the case • law review • lawyer's trust account • lead counsel • legislative intent • liability • libel • link • liquidated da
igation • loaded • long-arm jurisdiction • lose • maintenance • malice aforethought • malicious prosecution • malpractice insurance • manual labor • making a
arriage • marrone • mason • matlock, ben • maundering • mcnaughton Rule • mendacity • mens rea • merely • minnesota twins, the • monopoly • mortgage
e • multi-state • navigable waters • negligence • new york • new york lawyers • ninth amendment • no-knock warrant • not-for-profit corporation • nutshell •
um • objection • obscenity • offer • old bailey • oligarchy • originalist • paternity • paternity test • palimony • penultimate • perspicuity • pike test • plea b
essey v. ferguson • potter, stewart • poverty law • pornography • prevarication • product liability • professional responsibility • prior inconsistent statement
raint • prolix • public interest law • public interest lawyer • punitive damages • quantum meruit • quash • quarter section • question presented • quid pro quo
m deed • rainmaker • rational basis test • rejection • remand • residuum • residuum rule • res ipsa loquitor • res judicata • respondent superior • responsible
• rule against perpetuities • screw • screw-the-pooch • second amendment • sentence • separation of powers • settlement • seventh amendment • sinking
eenth amendment • sixth amendment • slander • solicitation • spendthrift • stare decisis • stages of marriage • statute • statutes of frauds • street lawyer •
struction • strict scrutiny • sub rosa • substantive due process • sudden heat of passion • summer associate • taylor law • take it upstairs • taxation • tenth a
nt • think-they-know-it-all • third amendment • tickle • title insurance • tort • to wit • traduce • trespass • trust • ultimate • unambiguous • unconstitutional • u
mercial code • unique • united states supreme court • unjust enrichment • usury • usufruct • vagrant • verified pleading • very • waiver • warhorse • war
ress • warranty, implied • warranty period • ways-and-means • webster, daniel • west publishing • whole-life insurance • wirt, william • withholding • yield •
kel • zealous representation • zone of interest test • zoning • absence of malice • accessory • accomplice • acquit • act of god • action • activist judge • actu
ministrative law • admiralty law • agent • albatross • alimony • alternative pleading • amnesty • ambulance chaser • antitrust laws • appeal • arbitrary and
s • armed and dangerous • as is • assumpsit • attorney • b.m.w • bad debt • bait and switch • bankrupt • bankruptcy •bar •bar review course • basis • be
t evidence rule • big gun •bilious •billable hour •birdie •black acre • black letter law • blue book • bogart • bogie • boiler plate • bonus • book •boot •booty
be • bust •busted • c.a.f.o. •calendar call • chain • child support •churning the file • circumstantial evidence •citation • class action • clearly • clients • c
• coffee • comparative negligence • compensatory damages • consideration • constitutional law • contract • contributory negligence • contumacious •co
• corpus delicti • counselor • creditor • cross examination • dead file • dead man's acts • deceit • deep pocket • de minimis non curat lex • demurrer • dep
erogatory clause • devil's dictionary • dictionary, law • directed verdict • disclosure • divorce • dormant commerce clause • dorr's Rebellion • double billing • d
pardy • due process • dying declaration • e.s.o.p. employee share ownership plan • eagle absence of malice • accessory • accomplice • acquit • act of god •
stivist judge • actus reus • administrative law • admiralty law • agent • albatross • alimony • alternative pleading • amnesty • ambulance chaser • antitrust l
eal • arbitrary and capricious • armed and dangerous • as is • assumpsit • attorney • b.m.w • bad debt • bait and switch • bankrupt • bankruptcy •bar •bar r
irdie • basis • bench • best evidence rule • big gun •bilious •billable hour •birdie •black acre • black letter law • blue book • bogart • bogie • boiler plate • b
k •boot •booty • bork •bribe • bust •busted • c.a.f.o. •calendar call • chain • child support •churning the file • circumstantial evidence •citation • class ac
rly • clients • closing costs • coffee • comparative negligence • compensatory damages • consideration • constitutional law • contract • contributory neglige
umacious •corporation • corpus delicti • counselor • creditor • cross examination • dead file • dead man's acts • deceit • deep pocket • de minimis non cura
urrer • deposition • derogatory clause • devil's dictionary • dictionary, law • directed verdict • disclosure • divorce • dormant commerce clause • dorr's Rebe
ble billing • double jeopardy • due process • dying declaration • e.s.o.p. employee share ownership plan • eagle • economic development program • ego •
andment •ejuration • entitlement • equal protection clause • equity • escheat •estate • estop • estoppel, equitable • ethics • evidence, laws of / rules of • e
rance • exclusionary rule • exculpatory evidence rule • exhaustion of remedies • ex-wife/ex-husband • face time • fair • fair use doctrine • fairway • false ar
ral judge • federalism • federal witness protection program • federalist society • fifth amendment • filibuster • first amendment • floating crap game • four
andment • fourth amendment • force majeure • franking privilege •fraud • frivolous • fruit of the poisonous tree • fundamental right • garden • general denial •
ader • gift causa mortis • gift tax • gloss • good samaritan statues • got my papers! • great compromise • graft • gross • guarantee clause • guilt • h.a.p. • h
us • habitability • habitability, warrantee of • hack • hand, Learned • harmless error • harvard law • hassle • hazardous • hazardous waste • headnote • hea
oom • hereinabove, hereinafter, heretofore • he said, she said • homicide • hornbook • hose • hundred weight • hung jury • ill fame • immoral • impedin

GREASEY, SHEEN, AND DRUM, P.C.
ENVIRONMENTAL LAWYERS
SPECIALIZING IN SUPERFUND
AND TOXIC TORT DEFENSE

garden. 1. A small piece of land appropriated to raising a variety of herbs, fruit, flowers, or vegetables. 2. An example of a supposed legal term of art defined in a law dictionary for which a student entering law school will squander nearly one hundred dollars.

general denial. The preferred response to a pleading that contains a complete and accurate recitation of facts comprising a valid cause of action.

gerrymander. The fair and democratic method of drawing the lines of electoral districts. In this system, called "putting the fox in charge of the hen house," the party in control of a legislative body draws the boundaries of the districts. Hence, in our democracy, the turnover rate for incumbent legislative officials is lower than it was in the single-party Soviet Union.

Gibbons v. Ogden, **22 U.S. (9 Wheat) 1 (1824).** A dispute over interstate commerce that caused a great furor before it was heard, but which the Supreme Court decided on the grounds least likely to offend anyone—and therefore least likely to provide any meaningful guidance for the future.

Gideon v. Wainwright, **372 U.S. 335 (1963).** The ultimate decision in a line of cases that transformed the Sixth Amendment right to be represented by an attorney in a criminal proceeding into an entitlement to be provided an attorney at the taxpayers' expense.

gift causa mortis. "Give back my stuff! I was only being generous because I thought I was about to croak."

gift tax. No good deed goes unpunished—especially if the government finds out about it.

gloss. Judges shining us on.

Good Samaritan statues. Laws intended to protect people who aid others from lawsuits. As with most things done by lawyers, the protection is not absolute. Therefore, the statutes actually provide a road map of how to sue people who fail to succeed in a rescue attempt. On the other hand, one who sees another in imminent peril and does nothing faces no liability at all. This is yet another reason for people to hate lawyers.

got my papers. A phrase referring to walking papers, or notice of dismissal, usually received after six to eight years working like a galley slave in a fool's hope of becoming a partner in a prestigious law firm. Failure to make partner ends any hope of having a fruitful career. The terminated associate will not find a job with any firm that does meaningful work for respectable clients.

graft. A bonus program for elected officials and their friends and supporters. The level of compensation under this system rises in direct proportion to the status of the official.

Great Compromise. The bargain struck in Philadelphia that ended the stalemate between representatives of small states and large states regarding the system of representation in the proposed national government, creating the bicameral system with proportional representation in the House of Representatives and two senators from each state, no matter how small and out of the mainstream their populations might be.

gross. 1. In environmental law, gross refers to contamination by petroleum or hazardous wastes so severe that the pollutant saturates the environmental medium rather than merely dissolving or diffusing. Imagine chemicals running out of the sides of a pit excavated in a contaminated area, causing the workers to declare, "Man, that's gross!" 2. In tax and finance law, gross refers to the total of some amount before deduction of "expenses" that allow business owners to live like kings while reporting incomes below the poverty level. 3. In criminal law, gross refers to the personal hygiene of indigent defendants and those who have been incarcerated for a significant length of time.

Groves v. Slaughter, **40 U.S. (15 Pet.) 449 (1841).** The case in which the United States Supreme Court held that the federal courts are not required to apply a state statute or constitution if doing so would be politically inconvenient for the federal government or the political party responsible for appointing a majority of the Supreme Court justices.

Grundy, Felix. Attorney General of the United States from 1838 to 1839. He hatched the theory that the Africans who commandeered the ship *L' Amistad* from their kidnappers were actually property that the United States should return to the kidnappers. This ignored Spanish law, which prohibited the importation of slaves to Cuba, from whence the Africans had fled, and New York State law, which declared all persons entering the state to be free.

guarantee clause. One of several dead letters in the United States Constitution, this one proclaims that the federal government will guarantee a republican form of government in each of the states of the United States. Since Dorr's Rebellion, the courts have eschewed enforcement of this clause, resulting in oligarchy in New York and anarchy in California.

guilt. A state of mind absent from the guilty.

debt • bait and switch • bankrupt • bankruptcy •bar •bar review course • basis • bench • best evidence rule • big gun •bilious •billable hour •birdie •black
nck letter law • blue book • bogart • bogie • boiler plate • bonus • book •boot •booty • bork •bribe • bust • busted • c.a.f.o. •calendar call • chain • child
rning the file • circumstantial evidence •citation • class action • clearly • clients • closing costs • coffee • comparative negligence • compensatory damag
sideration • constitutional law • contract • contributory negligence • contumacious •corporation • corpus delicti • counselor • creditor • cross examination • dea
ad man's acts • deceit • deep pocket • de minimis non curat lex • demurrer • deposition • derogatory clause • devil's dictionary • dictionary, law • directed ve
sclosure • divorce • dormant commerce clause • dorr's Rebellion • double billing • double jeopardy • due process • dying declaration • e.s.o.p. employee share o
plan • eagle • economic development program • ego • eighth amendment •ejuration • entitlement • equal protection clause • equity • escheat •estate • es
opel, equitable • ethics • evidence, laws of / rules of • excited utterance • exclusionary rule • exculpatory evidence rule • exhaustion of remedies • ex-wi
and • face time • fair • fair use doctrine • fairway • false arrest • federal judge • federalism • federalism • federal witness protection program • federalist so
amendment • fifteenth amendment • filibuster • first amendment • floating crap game • fourteenth amendment • fourth amendment • force majeure • fra
lege •fraud • frivolous • fruit of the poisonous tree • fundamental right • garden • general denial • gerrymander • gift causa mortis • gift tax • gloss • good sa
statues • got my papers! • great compromise • graft • gross • guarantee clause • guilt • h.a.p. • habeas corpus • habitability • habitability, warrantee of • h
l, Learned • harmless error • harvard law • hassle • hazardous • hazardous waste • headnote • hearsay • heirloom • hereinabove, hereinafter, heretofore • he
said • homicide • hornbook • hose • hundred weight • hung jury • ill fame • immoral • impediment to marriage • import-export clause • imputed negligence • imp
corporation by reference • income • inchoate • indemnity • indigent • inevitable discovery rule • infancy • internal Revenue code • internal Revenue service •
al property • interstate commerce • ipso facto • irrelevant • jack • jeopardy • judicial review • jump • jail • jailhouse lawyer • joint and several liability • journa
dge • judgment • judgment not withstanding the verdict • jurisprudence • jury • jury instructions • jury wheel • just compensation • justice • justification • k
uver-cellars act • kentucky rule • kick • kickback • kilo • kiting • kleptomania • knock and announce • know • know-it-all • known-heirs • laches, estoppel by •
ract • lapse in judgement • law • law of the case • law review • lawyer's trust account • lead counsel • legislative intent • liability • libel • link • liquidated dam
gation • loaded • long-arm jurisdiction • lose • maintenance • malice aforethought • malicious prosecution • malpractice insurance • manual labor • making a r
irriage • marrone • mason • matlock, ben • maundering • mcnaughton Rule • mendacity • mens rea • merely • minnesota twins, the • monopoly • mortgage
• multi-state • navigable waters • negligence • new york • new york lawyers • ninth amendment • no-knock warrant • not-for-profit corporation • nutshell •
m • objection • obscenity • offer • old bailey • oligarchy • onginalist • paternity • paternity test • palimony • penultimate • perspicuity • pike test • plea b
nssey v ferguson • potter, stewart • poverty law • pornography • prevarication • product liability • professional responsibility • prior inconsistent statement •
aint • prolix • public interest law • public interest lawyer • punitive damages • quantum meruit • quash • quarter section • question presented • quid pro quo •
h deed • rainmaker • rational basis test • rejection • remand • residuum • residuum rule • res ipsa loquitor • res judicata • respondent superior • responsible o
• rule against perpetuities • screw • screw-the-pooch • second amendment • sentence • separation of powers • settlement • seventh amendment • sinking f
enth amendment • sixth amendment • slander • solicitation • spendthrift • stare decisis • stages of marriage • statute • statutes of frauds • street lawyer •
truction • strict scrutiny • sub rosa • substantive due process • sudden heat of passion • summer associate • taylor law • take it upstairs • taxation • tenth am
t • think-they-know-it-all • third amendment • tickle • title insurance • tort • to wit • traduce • trespass • trust • ultimate • unambiguous • unconstitutional • un
rnal code • unique • united states supreme court • unjust enrichment • usury • usufruct • vagrant • verified pleading • very • waiver • warhorse • war
ess • warranty, implied • warranty period • ways-and-means • webster, daniel • west publishing • whole-life insurance • wirt, william • withholding • yield •
kel • zealous representation • zone of interest test • zoning • absence of malice • accessory • accomplice • acquit • act of god • action • activist judge • actus
ministrative law • admiralty law • agent • albatross • alimony • alternative pleading • amnesty • ambulance chaser • antitrust laws • appeal • arbitrary and
s • armed and dangerous • as is • assumpsit • attorney • b.m.w. • bad debt • bait and switch • bankrupt • bankruptcy •bar •bar review course • basis • bee
evidence rule • big gun •bilious •billable hour •birdie •black acre • black letter law • blue book • bogart • bogie • boiler plate • bonus • book •boot •booty
ie • bust • busted • c.a.t.o. •calendar call • chain • child support •churning the file • circumstantial evidence •citation • class action • clearly • clients • cl
s • coffee • comparative negligence • compensatorFy damages • consideration • constitutional law • contract • contributory negligence • contumacious •cor
s • corpus delicti • counselor • creditor • cross examination • dead file • dead man's acts • deceit • deep pocket • de minimis non curat lex • demurrer • depo
ogatory clause • devil's dictionary • dictionary, law • directed verdict • disclosure • divorce • dormant commerce clause • dorr's Rebellion • double billing • de
ardy • due process • dying declaration • e.s.o.p. employee share ownership plan • eagle absence of malice • accessory • accomplice • acquit • act of god • al
tivist judge • actus reus • administrative law • admiralty law • agent • albatross • alimony • alternative pleading • amnesty • ambulance chaser • antitrust la
al • arbitrary and capricious • armed and dangerous • as is • assumpsit • attorney • b.m.w. • bad debt • bait and switch • bankrupt • bankruptcy •bar • bar re
se • basis • bench • best evidence rule • big gun •bilious •billable hour •birdie •black acre • black letter law • blue book • bogart • bogie • boiler plate • bo
•boot •booty • bork •bribe • bust •busted • c.a.t.o. •calendar call • chain • child support •churning the file • circumstantial evidence •citation • class act
ly • clients • closing costs • coffee • comparative negligence • compensatory damages • consideration • constitutional law • contract • contributory negligen
umacious •corporation • corpus delicti • counselor • creditor • cross examination • dead file • dead man's acts • deceit • deep pocket • de minimis non curat
rrer • deposition • derogatory clause • devil's dictionary • dictionary, law • directed verdict • disclosure • divorce • dormant commerce clause • dorr's Rebell
le billing • double jeopardy • due process • dying declaration • e.s.o.p employee share ownership plan • eagle • economic development program • ego • e
ndment •ejuration • entitlement • equal protection clause • equity • escheat •estate • estop • estoppel, equitable • ethics • evidence, laws of / rules of • ex
ance • exclusionary rule • exculpatory evidence rule • exhaustion of remedies • ex-wife/ex-husband • face time • fair • fair use doctrine • fairway • false arr
al judge • federalism • federal witness protection program • federalist society • fifth amendment • filibuster • first amendment • floating crap game • fourte
dment • fourth amendment • force majeure • franking privilege •fraud • frivolous • fruit of the poisonous tree • fundamental right • garden • general denial • g
ler • gift causa mortis • gift tax • gloss • good samaritan statues • got my papers! • great compromise • graft • gross • guarantee clause • guilt • h.a.p. • ho
us • habitability • habitability, warrantee of • hack • hand, Learned • harmless error • harvard law • hassle • hazardous • hazardous waste • headnote • hear
hereinabove, hereinafter, heretofore • he said, she said • homicide • hornbook • hose • hundred weight • hung jury • ill fame • immoral • impedimen

HATCHET, JOBS, AND BULL
LITIGATORS

NOAH BULL, ESQ., SENIOR PARTNER
SPECIALIST IN DEPOSITIONS AND
CROSS-EXAMINATIONS

habeas corpus. Any one of several writs formerly issued by courts of common law directing that a person appear before a particular court for various purposes. What most people think of as habeas corpus today is the writ habeas corpus ad subjiciendum, which commands one who holds another in custody to present the prisoner before the court. This contraction and resulting imprecision occurred when the slacker who drafted the United States Constitution was too lazy to write out the whole term and merely called it habeas corpus.

habitability. A subjective matter, particularly for spouses who come from varying socio-economic backgrounds. Take a well-heeled, city-reared spouse to your grandfather's rustic fishing camp in the mountains and you may learn that the cabin in which you lived for entire summers is not fit to inhabit for a weekend.

habitability, warranty of. The ill-advised assurance to your spouse that (s)he will love the rustic mountain cabin at which you plan to spend a surprise romantic getaway.

hack. 1. Someone who is paid more than you for doing less work. 2. It isn't what you know. It isn't who you know. It is how much you donated to winning political campaigns.

Hand, Learned. This persevering man overcame the stigma of a name that included an adjective and a body part to become one of the great jurists in American history.

H.A.P. Abbreviation for Hazardous Air Pollutant. It is used as a word—hap—in casual conversation among engineers and environmental attorneys. Since nobody has found a pollutant that does not pose a hazard of some type, this term should be "Really Hazardous Air Pollutant." However, engineers and lawyers are generally older upper-middle-class professionals who do not like "rhap."

harmless error. A judicial mistake in a proceeding—particularly a trial—that allows the loser to drive up the cost and inconvenience of litigation through motions and appeals without actually reversing the result.

Harvard Law. The Holy See of secular humanism.

hassle. Any task for which you are not being paid $400 per hour or that is so annoying you would forgo the $400 per hour if you could get out of the job without being fired, demoted, or disbarred.

hate crime. A crime of violence or intimidation committed as an expression of the perpetrator's invidious prejudice against a social or racial characteristic of the victim. Not all jurisdictions have codified hate crimes as distinctly punishable actions. Opponents of hate crimes legislation argue that prosecuting hate crimes punishes people for politically incorrect thoughts. They also claim that hate crimes may easily be imputed from slurs or even jokes unrelated to the crime or from statements made in the heat of anger brought on by factors other than prejudice. On the other hand, the various degrees of homicide currently recognized by law are distinguished largely by the mens rea of the perpetrator—e.g., sudden heat of passion, malice aforethought, etc. But what it really boils down to is this: Is it really a tragedy if an asshole who beats the hell out of someone does an extra five to ten in jail?

hazardous. Being in a condition likely to cause harm. To a tort lawyer, this describes the state of the world and all the things in it.

hazardous waste. A material defined by chemical characteristics and factors such as pH, ignitability, acute toxicity, and other traits that only chemists and chemical engineers can ascertain. This was done because engineers and chemists wanted to join lawyers and bankers in bilking money from real estate transactions.

headnote. A statement in which Thomson West Publishing Company's editors explain a one-hundred-page decision in one hundred words.

hearsay. 1. An out-of-court statement repeated in testimony to prove the truth of the matter reportedly contained in the statement. 2. The news. *See he said, she said.*

heirloom. One man's treasure is another man's garage sale waiting to happen.

hereinabove, hereinafter, heretofore. "Somewhere else in this huge boring document, I wrote something relevant that I'm too lazy to repeat, and I know the readers probably will not look for it to confirm its applicability to the statement in which I cite myself, so I can stretch the truth with relative impunity."

he said, she said. 1. A case in which the only evidence comes from witnesses who contradict each other's testimony. 2. The format of most modern news reporting because media conglomerates have abandoned fact finding and turned to contrived interpersonal conflict as a means of increasing their ratings and circulation.

homicide. The killing of one human being by another. Although once presumed to be an unlawful act, it is now regarded as a benevolent deed that frees the perpetrator from unnecessary inconvenience and releases the decedent from the discomforts associated with life.

hornbook. A nonprescription sleep aid.

hose. To exercise one's discretion in a forthright or legitimate manner that places someone in a position of disadvantage or loss.

"The cop arrested me for doing sixty in a school zone while smoking a joint."

"Oh, man, you were hosed."

hundred weight. A mass measurement in the English or imperial system containing—I kid you not—112 pounds. Which is why sane people use the metric system.

hung jury. How would anyone know?

hyperbole. An exaggerated claim based on a misrepresentation of fact. This has become the most common part of speech used in legal parlance. "Defendant raced through the village with utter disregard for the consequences of his wild actions" translates to "Defendant drove 35 miles per hour in a 30 mile per hour speed zone." Most people call this bullshit.

debt • bait and switch • bankrupt • bankruptcy •bar •bar review course • basis • bench • best evidence rule • big gun •bilious •billable hour •birdie •black
ck letter law • blue book • bogart • bogie • boiler plate • bonus • book • boot •booty • bork • bribe • bust •busted • c.a.f.o. •calendar call • chain • child sup
ning the file • circumstantial evidence •citation • class action • clearly • clients • closing costs • coffee • comparative negligence • compensatory damag
deration • constitutional law • contract • contributory negligence • contumacious •corporation • corpus delicti • counselor • creditor • cross examination • dea
d man's acts • deceit • deep pocket • de minimis non curat lex • demurrer • deposition • derogatory clause • devil's dictionary • dictionary, law • directed ve
closure • divorce • dormant commerce clause • dorr's Rebellion • double billing • double jeopardy • due process • dying declaration • e.s o p. employee share ov
plan • eagle • economic development program • ego • eighth amendment •ejuration • entitlement • equal protection clause • equity • escheat •estate • est
pel, equitable • ethics • evidence, laws of / rules of • excited utterance • exclusionary rule • exculpatory evidence rule • exhaustion of remedies • ex-wife
and • face time • fair • fair use doctrine • fairway • false arrest • federal judge • federalism • federalism • federal witness protection program • federalist so
h amendment • fifteenth amendment • filibuster • first amendment • floating crap game • fourteenth amendment • fourth amendment • force majeure • fran
ege •fraud • frivolous • fruit of the poisonous tree • fundamental right • garden • general denial • gerrymander • gift causa mortis • gift tax • gloss • good sa
tatues • got my papers! • great compromise • graft • gross • guarantee clause • guilt • h.a.p. • habeas corpus • habitability • habitability, warrantee of •
Learned • harmless error • harvard law • hassle • hazardous • hazardous waste • headnote • hearsay • heirloom • hereinabove, hereinafter, heretofore • he
aid • homicide • hornbook • hose • hundred weight • hung jury • ill fame • immoral • impediment to marriage • import-export clause • imputed negligence • imp
orporation by reference • income • inchoate • indemnity • indigent • inevitable discovery rule • infancy • internal Revenue code • internal Revenue service •
al property • interstate commerce • ipso facto • irrelevant • jack • jeopardy • judicial review • jump • jail • jailhouse lawyer • joint and several liability • journa
age • judgment • judgment not withstanding the verdict • jurisprudence • jury • jury instructions • jury wheel • just compensation • justice • justification • k
ver-cellars act • kentucky rule • kick • kickback • kilo • kiting • kleptomania • knock and announce • know • know-it-all • known-heirs • laches, estoppel by •
act • lapse in judgement • law • law of the case • law review • lawyer's trust account • lead counsel • legislative intent • liability • libel • link • liquidated dam
ation • loaded • long-arm jurisdiction • lose • maintenance • malice aforethought • malicious prosecution • malpractice insurance • manual labor • making a rel
riage • marrone • mason • matlock, ben • maundering • mcnaughton Rule • mendacity • mens rea • merely • minnesota twins, the • monopoly • mortgage ir
• multi-state • navigable-waters • negligence • new york • new york lawyers • ninth amendment • no-knock warrant • not-for-profit corporation • nutshell • ol
n • objection • obscenity • offer • old bailey • oligarchy • originalist • paternity • paternity test • palimony • penultimate • perspicuity • pike test • plea bar
ssey v. ferguson • potter, stewart • poverty law • pomography • prevarication • product liability • professional responsibility • prior inconsistent statement •
int • prolix • public interest law • public interest lawyer • punitive damages • quantum meruit • quash • quarter section • question presented • quid pro quo •
deed • rainmaker • rational basis test • rejection • remand • residuum • residuum rule • res ipsa loquitor • res judicata • respondent superior • responsible of
• rule against perpetuities • screw • screw-the-pooch • second amendment • sentence • separation of powers • settlement • seventh amendment • sinking fu
nth amendment • sixth amendment • slander • solicitation • spendthrift • stare decisis • stages of marriage • statute • statutes of frauds • street lawyer • si
ruction • strict scrutiny • sub rosa • substantive due process • sudden heat of passion • summer associate • taylor law • take it upstairs • taxation • tenth am
• think-they-know-it-all • third amendment • tickle • title insurance • tort • to wit • traduce • trespass • trust • ultimate • unambiguous • unconstitutional • unne
ercial code • unique • united states supreme court • unjust enrichment • usury • usufruct • vagrant • verified pleading • very • waiver • warhorse • warra
ss • warranty, implied • warranty period • ways-and-means • webster, daniel • west publishing • whole-life insurance • witt, william • withholding • yield •
el • zealous representation • zone of interest test • zoning • absence of malice • accessory • accomplice • acquit • act of god • action • activist judge • actus
inistrative law • admiralty law • agent • albatross • alimony • alternative pleading • amnesty • ambulance chaser • antitrust laws • appeal • arbitrary and c
• armed and dangerous • as is • assumpsit • attorney • b.m.w. • bad debt • bait and switch • bankrupt • bankruptcy •bar •bar review course • basis • ben
evidence rule • big gun •bilious •billable hour •birdie •black acre • black letter law • blue book • bogart • bogie • boiler plate • bonus • book •boot •booty •
e • bust •busted • c.a.f o. •calendar call • chain • child support •churning the file • circumstantial evidence •citation • class action • clearly • clients • clo
• coffee • comparative negligence • compensatorfy damages • consideration • constitutional law • contract • contributory negligence • contumacious •corp
corpus delicti • counselor • creditor • cross examination • dead file • dead man's acts • deceit • deep pocket • de minimis non curat lex • demurrer • depos
gatory clause • devil's dictionary • dictionary, law • directed verdict • disclosure • divorce • dormant commerce clause • dorr's Rebellion • double billing • do
dy • due process • dying declaration • e.s.o.p. employee share ownership plan • eagle absence of malice • accessory • accomplice • acquit • act of god • ac
vist judge • actus reus • administrative law • admiralty law • agent • albatross • alimony • alternative pleading • amnesty • ambulance chaser • antitrust law
al • arbitrary and capricious • armed and dangerous • as is • assumpsit • attorney • b m.w. • bad debt • bait and switch • bankrupt • bankruptcy •bar •bar rev
e • basis • bench • best evidence rule • big gun •bilious •billable hour •birdie •black acre • black letter law • blue book • bogart • bogie • boiler plate • bon
•boot •booty • bork • bribe • bust •busted • c.a f.o. •calendar call • chain • child support •churning the file • circumstantial evidence •citation • class actic
y • clients • closing costs • coffee • comparative negligence • compensatory damages • consideration • constitutional law • contract • contributory negligen
macious •corporation • corpus delicti • counselor • creditor • cross examination • dead file • dead man's acts • deceit • deep pocket • de minimis non curat l
rrer • deposition • derogatory clause • devil's dictionary • dictionary, law • directed verdict • disclosure • divorce • dormant commerce clause • dorr's Rebellie
a billing • double jeopardy • due process • dying declaration • e.s.o.p. employee share ownership plan • eagle • economic development program • ego • ei
dment •ejuration • entitlement • equal protection clause • equity • escheat •estate • estop • estoppel, equitable • ethics • evidence, laws of / rules of • exc
nce • exclusionary rule • exculpatory evidence rule • exhaustion of remedies • ex-wife/ex-husband • face time • fair • fair use doctrine • fairway • false arre
al judge • federalism • federal witness protection program • federalist society • fifth amendment • filibuster • first amendment • floating crap game • fourtee
dment • fourth amendment • force majeure • franking privilege •fraud • frivolous • fruit of the poisonous tree • fundamental right • garden • general denial • ge
r • gift causa mortis • gift tax • gloss • good samaritan statues • got my papers! • great compromise • graft • gross • guarantee clause • guilt • h.a.p. • hat
r • habitability, habitability, warrantee of • hack • hand, Learned • harmless error • harvard law • hassle • hazardous • hazardous waste • headnote • hearsa

IZZI, WRIGHT, ORE, KNOT, & CO.
DISCRETE PRIVATE INVESTIGATIONS
DIVORCE, EMBEZZLEMENT, FRAUD,
AND PRENUPTIAL ASSURANCE

"I'll admit it for what it is worth." A phrase used by judges in bench trials and administrative proceedings in which the judge acts as both fact finder and arbiter of the law. The phrase has a bifurcated meaning. "I'll admit it" means the feckless judge is about to let irrelevant, unsubstantiated, or prejudicial material into the factual record of the proceeding over the objection of opposing counsel. "For what it's worth," means the judge knows that the evidence should be excluded, and he intends to disregard it when making his findings of fact. Trial judges justify this by saying it protects their determinations from appellate courts that exist to reverse determinations of law but cannot easily disregard the findings of fact made at the trial level. This is wonderful—unless you are paying for the lawyer, the transcripts, and other expenses caused by the pointless extension of the proceeding.

ill fame. An oxymoron in American culture.

immoral. Being outside the realm of acceptable conduct in society, but likely to get a lot of attention, command high ratings on daytime television and cable networks, and sell tens of thousands of DVDs at $24.95 each.

impeach. To humiliate a witness for fun and profit.

impediment to marriage. Good luck or good sense.

Import-Export Clause. Article I, Section 10, Clause 2 of the United States Constitution prohibits states from taxing imports and exports without congressional consent. However, the Supreme Court rendered this clause inoperable by discovery of the so-called Dormant Commerce Clause.

imputed negligence. The hand that picks the deep pocket.

inchoate. Being incomplete or unperfected, which pretty much describes every human endeavor.

income. The fruits of labor or investment produced to support the government, a portion of which an individual might retain for his or her own subsistence.

incorporation by reference. The ultimate tool of composition for the lazy attorney-author. The attorney-author refers to a document by another author without investing the labor to actually transcribe it. This saves the author-attorney the bother of writing his own document and places the burden of finding the source document on the reader.

indemnity. A financial security blanket provided by someone else. Like the security blanket you had as a child, it makes you feel better as long as things are good, but when the monsters from your closet come after you, you'd better hope Mom and Dad are around to save you.

indigent. Having too little wealth or income to provide for one's own subsistence, as with public defenders, assistant district attorneys, and public interest lawyers.

ineffective assistance of counsel. A defense raised by rote in appeals of criminal convictions claiming that the convict's lawyer was so bad that the trial violated the Sixth Amendment right to a fair trial. The erstwhile defendant must overcome a strong presumption that his lawyer acted reasonably in light of professional standards. It is standard practice for criminals, even those being handled by assigned counsel, to get a new lawyer to handle their appeals so they can include a claim of ineffective assistance of counsel. In smaller jurisdictions, this means every criminal defense lawyer has repeatedly informed the appellate courts that every other criminal defense attorney in that area is an incompetent moron. Therefore, the courts will be hard pressed to ever find an attorney who didn't live up to the standards of the profession.

inevitable discovery rule. Evidence that might be rendered inadmissible because it was obtained by illegal means may be admitted if the prosecutor can successfully compose a few new verses for "This is the House that Jack Built."

infancy. Most people think of infancy as being that period of a child's life from birth to toddler. Lawyers, judges, and legislators observed the behavior of teenagers and realized that although vocabulary and physical dexterity increased in (most) children, self-control, foresight, and emotional maturity remain unchanged or regress from age 1 to age 18.

intellectual property. A fiction of law that blesses the creative among us and renders ownership of our imaginary worlds more valuable than gold or land.

Internal Revenue Code. The collective laws of the United States government concerning manipulation of individual behavior to reward sloth and punish invest-ment, hard work, and personal thrift. Incidentally, these laws generate money for the treasury.

Internal Revenue Service. The federal bureaucracy charged with administering the Internal Revenue Code, particularly the collection of taxes. Compliance is compulsory and enforcement involves interest,

69

penalties, fines, and imprisonment. "Ruthless, cold-hearted enforcers who take your money" described the Mafia too, so Congress settled on the name "Internal Revenue Service" to avoid confusion.

interstate commerce. 1. Any activity that *might* have some effect on the national economy *if* everyone in the nation engaged in the activity simultaneously. *See Wickard v. Filburn 317 U.S. 111 (1942)*. 2. Any activity that Congress wants to regulate.

ipso facto. Something proven by the fact in and of itself. If you have to say "ipso facto" the term doesn't apply to your situation. If it did, you would not need to explain it.

irrelevant. Not pertaining to an argument or its rational conclusion. Ironically, an inverse proportion exists between how intrinsically interesting a fact is and how relevant it will be to the application of the law in a particular case.

JOY & HOPE
ATTORNEYS AT LAW
YOUR ADOPTION SPECIALISTS

jack. 1. A recreational activity of male youths in which participants unlawfully take possession of an item by use of a firearm. This game is adapted to the habitat occupied by the devolved goons who practice it. In rural areas, it involves killing game at night with the aid of a light and a rifle. In urban areas, it involves the use of a handgun to convince people to surrender their vehicles. 2. What most young lawyers should expect to be paid.

jail. Exclusive public housing with lousy neighbors, no view, poor facilities, and one of the highest costs per square foot of any living space ever built—but slightly less violence and fewer drug dealers than the public housing that is available to the populace at large.

jailhouse lawyer. An incarcerated convict who—despite the demonstrable evidence of his lack of legal acumen—purports to know the law and dispenses legal advice to other inmates.

jeopardy. 1. The condition of a person facing threat of harm. 2. A condition to which criminals may expose their victims as often as they like, but which they are unlikely to confront in the justice system.

Johnson, Revardy. Daniel Webster with a southern accent.

join the choir. A phrase used in criminal law to describe a plea bargain pursuant to which a defendant agrees to sing the prosecutor's tune while testifying against his codefendants.

joint and several liability. The defendant with the most money gets hosed.

journalist's privilege. A judicial doctrine that authorizes reporters to use rumor and innuendo to ruin peoples' lives with impunity.

judgment. 1. An attribute one hopes to find in judges. 2. A court's decision and also the reasons stated therefore, although one may have little to do with the other.

judgment not withstanding the verdict. (Judgment non obstante verdicto or J.N.O.V.) A J.N.O.V. occurs when a gutless judge could have rendered a final decision in a case as a matter of law but gave the jury a chance to screw up instead. Once the jury makes the wrong decision, the judge must enter a judgment not withstanding the verdict.

judicial review. The rationalization by which judges convert their ideology into positive law.

juice. 1. Personal influence used to achieve a desired result outside legally or socially proscribed procedures. "Tell Eddie not to worry about that possession charge. The old man has some juice with the D.A." The problem with juice is that it isn't always reliable— e.g., "Eddie is doing three to five in Attica 'cause the old man didn't have enough juice." 2. The same as vig in bookmaking.

jump. To obtain a promotion by switching firms. The term particularly applies to associates in top New York firms.

jurisprudence. Something that exists only so long as we have prudent jurists.

jury. A group of select individuals sworn to glean a few kernels of truth from the wasted hours of lawyers' presentations.

jury instructions. A few minutes of oral directions from which a judge expects a jury to comprehend laws that he has studied and applied for his entire career.

jury wheel. A torture device used to separate qualified citizens from their families and inflict insufferable boredom upon them.

just compensation. The amount of money the government must pay when it confiscates private property. "Just compensation" means "just as little as we can get away with paying," and excludes considerations such as emotional attachment, the value of income that the property may produce, inability to obtain a similar parcel, or costs of relocation and re-establishing oneself.

justice. A term that formerly meant the proper application of law or the equitable allocation of rights and responsibilities among individuals. It now means "we want more money from the taxpayers."

justification. A good rationalization concocted by a lawyer after the fact for a client who committed an unlawful act, or failed to carry out a lawfully required duty, and got caught.

debt • bait and switch • bankrupt • bankruptcy •bar •bar review course • basis • bench • best evidence rule • big gun •bilious •billable hour •birdie •black
ck letter law • blue book • bogart • bogie • boiler plate • bonus • book •boot •booty • bork •bribe • bust •busted • c.a.f.o. •calendar call • chain • child sup
rning the file • circumstantial evidence •citation • class action • clearly • clients • closing costs • coffee • comparative negligence • compensatory damag
deration • constitutional law • contract • contributory negligence • contumacious •corporation • corpus delicti • counselor • creditor • cross examination • dead
d man's acts • deceit • deep pocket • de minimis non curat lex • demurrer • deposition • derogatory clause • devil's dictionary • dictionary, law • directed ve
losure • divorce • dormant commerce clause • dorr's Rebellion • double billing • double jeopardy • due process • dying declaration • e.s.o.p. employee share ow
plan • eagle • economic development program • ego • eighth amendment •ejuration • entitlement • equal protection clause • equity • escheat •estate • est
pel, equitable • ethics • evidence, laws of / rules of • excited utterance • exclusionary rule • exculpatory evidence rule • exhaustion of remedies • ex-wife
and • face time • fair • fair use doctrine • fairway • false arrest • federal judge • federalism • federalism • federal witness protection program • federalist so
h amendment • fifteenth amendment • filibuster • first amendment • floating crap game • fourteenth amendment • fourth amendment • force majeure • fran
age •fraud • frivolous • fruit of the poisonous tree • fundamental right • garden • general denial • gerrymander • gift causa mortis • gift tax • gloss • good sa
tatues • got my papers! • great compromise • graft • gross • guarantee clause • guilt • h.a.p. • habeas corpus • habitability • habitability, warrantee of • ha
Learned • harmless error • harvard law • hassle • hazardous • hazardous waste • headnote • hearsay • heirloom • hereinabove, hereinafter, heretofore • he s
aid • homicide • hornbook • hose • hundred weight • hung jury • ill fame • immoral • impediment to marriage • import-export clause • imputed negligence • impe
orporation by reference • income • inchoate • indemnity • indigent • inevitable discovery rule • infancy • internal Revenue code • internal Revenue service • i
al property • interstate commerce • ipso facto • irrelevant • jack • jeopardy • judicial review • jump • jail • jailhouse lawyer • joint and several liability • journa
ege • judgment • judgment not withstanding the verdict • jurisprudence • jury • jury instructions • jury wheel • just compensation • justice • justification • k.
ver-cellars act • kentucky rule • kick • kickback • kilo • kiting • kleptomania • knock and announce • know • know-it-all • known-heirs • laches, estoppel by •
act • lapse in judgement • law • law of the case • law review • lawyer's trust account • lead counsel • legislative intent • liability • libel • link • liquidated dam
ation • loaded • long-arm jurisdiction • lose • maintenance • malice aforethought • malicious prosecution • malpractice insurance • manual labor • making a re
riage • marrone • mason • matlock, ben • maundering • mcnaughten Rule • mendacity • mens rea • merely • minnesota twins, the • monopoly • mortgage in
• multi-state • navigable waters • negligence • new york • new york lawyers • ninth amendment • no-knock warrant • not-for-profit corporation • nutshell • o
n • objection • obscenity • offer • old bailey • oligarchy • onginalist • paternity • paternity test • palimony • penultimate • perspicuity • pike test • plea bas
ssey v. ferguson • potter, stewart • poverty law • pornography • prevarication • product liability • professional responsibility • prior inconsistent statement •
int • prolix • public interest law • public interest lawyer • punitive damages • quantum meruit • quash • quarter section • question presented • quid pro quo •
deed • rainmaker • rational basis test • rejection • remand • residuum • residuum rule • res ipsa loquitor • res judicata • respondent superior • responsible of
• rule against perpetuities • screw • screw-the-pooch • second amendment • sentence • separation of powers • settlement • seventh amendment • sinking fu
nth amendment • sixth amendment • slander • solicitation • spendthrift • stare decisis • stages of marriage • statute • statutes of frauds • street lawyer •
ruction • strict scrutiny • sub rosa • substantive due process • sudden heat of passion • summer associate • taylor law • take it upstairs • taxation • tenth am
• think-they-know-it-all • third amendment • tickle • title insurance • tort • to wit • traduce • trespass • trust • ultimate • unambiguous • unconstitutional • uni
nercial code • unique • united states supreme court • unjust enrichment • usury • usufruct • vagrant • verified pleading • very • waiver • warhorse • warra
ss • warranty, implied • warranty period • ways-and-means • webster, daniel • west publishing • whole-life insurance • wirt, william • withholding • yield •
el • zealous representation • zone of interest test • zoning • absence of malice • accessory • accomplice • acquit • act of god • action • activist judge • actus
ninistrative law • admiralty law • agent • albatross • alimony • alternative pleading • amnesty • ambulance chaser • antitrust laws • appeal • arbitrary and
• armed and dangerous • as is • assumpsit • attorney • b.m.w. • bad debt • bait and switch • bankrupt • bankruptcy • bar •bar review course • basis • bene
evidence rule • big gun •bilious •billable hour •birdie •black acre • black letter law • blue book • bogart • bogie • boiler plate • bonus • book •boot •booty •
ie • bust •busted • c.a.f.o. •calendar call • chain • child support •churning the file • circumstantial evidence •citation • class action • clearly • clients • clo
• coffee • comparative negligence • compensatorFy damages • consideration • constitutional law • contract • contributory negligence • contumacious •corp
• corpus delicti • counselor • creditor • cross examination • dead file • dead man's acts • deceit • deep pocket • de minimis non curat lex • demurrer • deposi
ogatory clause • devil's dictionary • dictionary, law • directed verdict • disclosure • divorce • dormant commerce clause • dorr's Rebellion • double billing • do
rdy • due process • dying declaration • e.s.o.p. employee share ownership plan • eagle absence of malice • accessory • accomplice • acquit • act of god • ae
vist judge • actus reus • administrative law • admiralty law • agent • albatross • alimony • alternative pleading • amnesty • ambulance chaser • antitrust law
al • arbitrary and capricious • armed and dangerous • as is • assumpsit • attorney • b.m.w. • bad debt • bait and switch • bankrupt • bankruptcy •bar • bar re
ie • basis • bench • best evidence rule • big gun •bilious •billable hour •birdie •black acre • black letter law • blue book • bogart • bogie • boiler plate • bon
•boot •booty • bork •bribe • bust •busted • c.a.f.o. •calendar call • chain • child support •churning the file • circumstantial evidence •citation • class acti
y • clients • closing costs • coffee • comparative negligence • compensatory damages • consideration • constitutional law • contract • contributory negligen
macious •corporation • corpus delicti • counselor • creditor • cross examination • dead file • dead man's acts • deceit • deep pocket • de minimis non curat l
rrer • deposition • derogatory clause • devil's dictionary • dictionary, law • directed verdict • disclosure • divorce • dormant commerce clause • dorr's Rebelli
e billing • double jeopardy • due process • dying declaration • e.s.o.p. employee share ownership plan • eagle • economic development program • ego • ei
dment •ejuration • entitlement • equal protection clause • equity • escheat •estate • estop • estoppel, equitable • ethics • evidence, laws of / rules of • exe
ance • exclusionary rule • exculpatory evidence rule • exhaustion of remedies • ex-wife/ex-husband • face time • fair • fair use doctrine • fairway • false arre
ial judge • federalism • federal witness protection program • federalist society • fifth amendment • filibuster • first amendment • floating crap game • fourtee
dment • fourth amendment • force majeure • franking privilege • fraud • frivolous • fruit of the poisonous tree • fundamental right • garden • general denial • g
er • gift causa mortis • gift tax • gloss • good samaritan statues • got my papers! • great compromise • graft • gross • guarantee clause • guilt • h.a.p. • ha
s • habitability • habitability, warrantee of • hack • hand, Learned • harmless error • harvard law • hassle • hazardous • hazardous waste • headnote • hearsa

The Kant-Barrett Law Firm
Employment Relations:
Age Discrimination,
Sexual Harassment,
and
Intentional Infliction
of Emotional Distress

k

K. 1. An abbreviation, usually used as a suffix, denoting that the amount preceding it should be multiplied by 1,000. This saves lawyers from writer's cramp when entering the amounts of their retainers into letters of engagement. 2. Shorthand for striking out in a baseball game. To "strike out" has become slang for a minor failure, and being too lazy to use slang, we now say K.

Kefauver-Cellars Act. Part of the federal micromanagement code. This particular law placed federal bureaucrats in charge of deciding if one business may buy another business or if two businesses may merge.

Kentucky rule. Trustees, liberally supplied with bourbon, consider all dividends to be income, whether received as cash or additional stock certificates.

kick. Short for kick the bucket. Something you hope clients do before you do so you can handle their estates.

kickback. A mafioso rebate.

kilo. A metric measurement of mass. If this is relevant to any of your clients' criminal cases, you have a good chance of quickly becoming rich or dead.

kiting. An investment method in which the investor writes and deposits checks back and forth among several accounts while using the lag time between when the check is credited in the depository account and when it is charged against the originating account to create the appearance that the originating account has more money than it does. Before instantaneous electronic fund transfers, this was a popular method for managing lawyers' trust accounts.

kleptomania. A psychological condition characterized by a compulsion to take other people's property or wealth. Fortunately, those afflicted with this condition can lead productive lives as politicians and United States Supreme Court justices. *Refer to Kelo vs. City of New London, 545 U.S. 469 (2005), 125 S Ct. 2655 (2005).*

knock and announce. A rule adopted from the children's game of cops-and-robbers that requires the police to shout "ready or not, here I come" before attempting to apprehend a criminal. There is no reciprocal rule stating that the criminal must shout "ollie-ollie-oxenfree" before running from the police.

know. Even to lawyers, know means know.

know-it-all. An individual who, at least within a particular discipline or specialty, knows all that a person can reasonably know. *See think-they-know-it-all.*

known heirs. The people whose existence and location are identifiable and who are entitled to receive property from the estate of a deceased person. The number of known heirs increases in proportion to the value of the estate.

LOCKE AND KEY, P.C.
CRIMINAL DEFENSE SPECIALISTS

laches, estoppel by. You snooze, you lose.

land contract. Progenitor of the rent-to-own system.

lapse in judgment. A decision made without full and rational thought, generally resulting in marriage, procreation, application to law school, or the leasing of luxury automobiles.

law. Philosophers have spent thousands of years debating what law is. Is it merely the sovereign's command, or maybe only a body of rules acceptable to a majority of the governed, or maybe any rule promulgated with due process? Fortunately, the deep thinkers at major publishers have had their say through their law dictionaries. By inserting one sentence from each philosopher's point of view into their definition, they have clarified the matter greatly. They finally cut to the heart of the matter and reveal to us that law is a body of rules that have legal force.

law office. 1. Formerly, a suite of rooms—preferably with raised hardwood panels, miles of bookshelves, and an assortment of expensive furniture—occupied by a lawyer or lawyers and supporting staff including secretaries, receptionists, and a mistress or two. 2. Currently, any place on the planet with cell phone coverage.

law of the case. The judicial rendition of that phrase so familiar to parents: "I said it, and I meant it!"

law review. 1. An honors organization that rewards the brightest and hardest working law students by requiring them to perform additional work to publish a compendium of articles by dithering egomaniacs. 2. A journal containing articles by students, law professors, judges, and elite practitioners who believe that the legal system will not endure without a full airing of their personal views on the law.

lawyer. The lawyer's place in society is analogous to the designated hitter in baseball. The American League uses designated hitters so pitchers can avoid the unpleasant task of attempting to hit the ball. In our politically correct society, anyone who directly disagrees with anyone else is considered a sexist-racist-homophobic-bigot, or simply a son of a bitch. So people hire lawyers to avoid the unpleasant task of talking honestly and reasonably with each other. Lawyers are designated sons of bitches.

lawyer's trust account. A checking account established so that a lawyer can spend other people's money.

lead counsel. When more than one attorney works on a particular case for a client, one emerges as the dominant specimen. This attorney is responsible for managing the work performed by the others and determining how much of the client's money will be squandered on frivolous activities.

legislative intent. A judge, acting as a medium, channels the spirits of the politicians who voted upon a statute that applies to a case. The judge asks what outcome the incorporeal politicos prefer, takes a roll call vote, and decides the case accordingly.

liability. The ore from which legal fees are—or have been—smelted.

libel. A false written statement that damages the reputation of another or subjects him to public scorn. Politicians call this campaigning.

link. A unit of linear measurement equaling 1/100th of a chain. *See chain.*

liquidated damages. The price of failure.

litigation. A formal dispute resolution process in which lawyers use the judicial system to maximize their fees.

loaded. 1. Bombed, blitzed, buzzed, drunk, hammered, pissed, toasted, zonked. 2. Rich. (Clients fitting the first description are more common than those fitting the second.)

long-arm jurisdiction. You don't live here, you don't have offices here, you don't do business here— you've never even been here. But you can be sued here. *Refer to International Shoe Co. v. Washington, 326 U.S. 310 (1945).*

lose. Something more lawyers should become accustomed to doing.

debt • bait and switch • bankrupt • bankruptcy • bar • bar review course • basis • bench • best evidence rule • big gun •bilious •billable hour •birdie •black a
letter law • blue book • bogart • bogie • boiler plate • bonus • book •boot •booty • bork •bribe • bust •busted • c.a.f.o. •calendar call • chain • child supp
ing the file • circumstantial evidence •citation • class action • clearly • clients • closing costs • coffee • comparative negligence • compensatory damage
aration • constitutional law • contract • contributory negligence • contumacious •corporation • corpus delicti • counselor • creditor • cross examination • dead
man's acts • deceit • deep pocket • de minimis non curat lex • demurrer • deposition • derogatory clause • devil's dictionary • dictionary, law • directed verdict
osure • divorce • dormant commerce clause • dorr's Rebellion • double billing • double jeopardy • due process • dying declaration • e.s.o.p. employee share own
an • eagle • economic development program • ego • eighth amendment •ejuration • entitlement • equal protection clause • equity • escheat •estate • esto
el, equitable • ethics • evidence, laws of / rules of • excited utterance • exclusionary rule • exculpatory evidence rule • exhaustion of remedies • ex-wife/
d • face time • fair • fair use doctrine • fairway • false arrest • federal judge • federalism • federalism • federal witness protection program • federalist soci
amendment • fifteenth amendment • filibuster • first amendment • floating crap game • fourteenth amendment • fourth amendment • force majeure • frank
e •fraud • frivolous • fruit of the poisonous tree • fundamental right • garden • general denial • gerrymander • gift causa mortis • gift tax • gloss • quod sam
atties • got my papers! • great compromise • graft • gross • guarantee clause • guilt • h.a.p. • habeas corpus • habitability • habitability, warrantee of • hac
earned • harmless error • harvard law • hassle • hazardous • hazardous waste • headnote • hearsay • heirloom • hereinabove, hereinafter, heretofore • he sa
d • homicide • hombook • hose • hundred weight • hung jury • ill fame • immoral • impediment to marriage • import-export clause • imputed negligence • impe
poration by reference • income • inchoate • indemnity • indigent • inevitable discovery rule • infancy • internal Revenue code • internal Revenue service • inil
property • interstate commerce • ipso facto • irrelevant • jack • jeopardy • judicial review • jump • jail • jailhouse lawyer • joint and several liability • journali
e • judgment • judgment not withstanding the verdict • jurisprudence • jury • jury instructions • jury wheel • just compensation • justice • justification • k.
ar-cellars act • kentucky rule • lick • kickback • kilo • kiting • kleptomania • knock and announce • know • know-it-all • known-heirs • laches, estoppel by • la
t • lapse in judgement • law • law of the case • law review • lawyer's trust account • lead counsel • legislative intent • liability • libel • link • liquidated dama
tion • loaded • long-arm jurisdiction • lose • maintenance • malice aforethought • malicious prosecution • malpractice insurance • manual labor • making a rec
age • malfone • mason • matlock, ben • maundering • mcnaughton Rule • mendacity • mens rea • merely • minnesota twins, the • monopoly • mortgage ins
multi-state • navigable waters • negligence • new york • new york lawyers • ninth amendment • no-knock warrant • not-for-profit corporation • nutshell • obi
• objection • obscenity • offer • old bailey • oligarchy • originalist • paternity • paternity test • palimony • penultimate • perspicuity • pike test • plea barg
ley v. ferguson • potter, stewart • poverty law • pornography • prevarication • product liability • professional responsibility • prior inconsistent statement • pi
nt • prolix • public interest law • public interest lawyer • punitive damages • quantum meruit • quash • quarter section • question presented • quid pro quo • qu
eed • rainmaker • rational basis test • rejection • remand • residuum • residuum rule • res ipsa loquitor • res judicata • respondent superior • responsible offi
ce against perpetuities • screw • screw-the-pouch • second amendment • sentence • separation of powers • settlement • seventh amendment • sinking fun
th amendment • sixth amendment • slander • solicitation • spendthrift • stare decisis • stages of marriage • statute • statutes of frauds • street lawyer • st
action • strict scrutiny • sub rosa • substantive due process • sudden heat of passion • summer associate • taylor law • take it upstairs • taxation • tenth ame
think-they-know-it-all • third amendment • tickle • title insurance • tort • to wit • traduce • trespass • trust • ultimate • unambiguous • unconstitutional • unifo
rcial code • unique • united states supreme court • unjust enrichment • usury • usufruct • vagrant • verified pleading • very • waiver • warhorse • warran
s • warranty, implied • warranty period • ways-and-means • webster, daniel • west publishing • whole-life insurance • writ, william • withholding • yield • yil
• zealous representation • zone of interest test • zoning • absence of malice • accessory • accomplice • acquit • act of god • action • activist judge • actus re
nistrative law • admiralty law • agent • albatross • alimony • alternative pleading • amnesty • ambulance chaser • antitrust laws • appeal • arbitrary and cap
armed and dangerous • as is • assumpsit • attorney • b.m.w. • bad debt • bait and switch • bankrupt • bankruptcy •bar •bar review course • basis • bench
idence rule • big gun •bilious •billable hour •birdie •black acre • black letter law • blue book • bogart • bogie • boiler plate • bonus • book •boot •booty • bi
• bust •busted • c.a.f.o. •calendar call • chain • child support •churning the file • circumstantial evidence •citation • class action • clearly • clients • clos
coffee • comparative negligence • compensatorFy damages • consideration • constitutional law • contract • contributory negligence • contumacious •corpo
corpus delicti • counselor • creditor • cross examination • dead file • dead man's acts • deceit • deep pocket • de minimis non curat lex • demurrer • deposit
gatory clause • devil's dictionary • dictionary, law • directed verdict • disclosure • divorce • dormant commerce clause • dorr's Rebellion • double billing • dou
ly • due process • dying declaration • e.s.o.p. employee share ownership plan • eagle absence of malice • accessory • accomplice • acquit • act of god • act
ist judge • actus reus • administrative law • admiralty law • agent • albatross • alimony • alternative pleading • amnesty • ambulance chaser • antitrust law
• arbitrary and capricious • armed and dangerous • as is • assumpsit • attorney • b.m.w. • bad debt • bait and switch • bankrupt • bankruptcy •bar •bar revi
• basis • bench • best evidence rule • big gun •bilious •billable hour •birdie •black acre • black letter law • blue book • bogart • bogie • boiler plate • bonu
boot •booty • bork •bribe • bust •busted • c.a.f.o •calendar call • chain • child support •churning the file • circumstantial evidence •citation • class action
• clients • closing costs • coffee • comparative negligence • compensatory damages • consideration • constitutional law • contract • contributory negligence
acious •corporation • corpus delicti • counselor • creditor • cross examination • dead file • dead man's acts • deceit • deep pocket • de minimis non curat la
er • deposition • derogatory clause • devil's dictionary • dictionary, law • directed verdict • disclosure • divorce • dormant commerce clause • dorr's Rebellion
billing • double jeopardy • due process • dying declaration • e.s.o.p. employee share ownership plan • eagle • economic development program • ego • eigl
ment •ejuration • entitlement • equal protection clause • equity • escheat •estate • estop • estoppel, equitable • ethics • evidence, laws of / rules of • exci
ce • exclusionary rule • exculpatory evidence rule • exhaustion of remedies • ex-wife/ex-husband • face time • fair • fair use doctrine • fairway • false arres
judge • federalism • federal witness protection program • federalist society • fifth amendment • filibuster • first amendment • floating crap game • fourtee
ment • fourth amendment • force majeure • franking privilege • fraud • frivolous • fruit of the poisonous tree • fundamental right • garden • general denial • ge
• gift causa mortis • gift tax • gloss • good samaritan statues • got my papers! • great compromise • graft • gross • guarantee clause • guilt • h.a.p. • habe
r • habitability • habitability, warrantee of • hack • hand. Learned • harmless error • harvard law • hassle • hazardous • hazardous waste • headnote • hearsa

MARCH AND BLAIR
LAWYERS WITH A SOCIAL CONSCIENCE

madonne. *Sicilian.* One of various legal terms of art used to encapsulate arguments in which the just and rational result is obvious, losing would create substantial injustice, and for which you cannot think of a single law or doctrine that supports your position. That is, "Judge, *madonne*!"

maintenance. A euphemism for monetary payments paid by one spouse (usually male) to the other. It was believed that because males have a predilection for mechanical tinkering and constant harping about oil changes, tire rotation, and radiator flushes, they would not complain about routine maintenance for former spouses.

making a record. Placing evidence before a court after all hope of winning the proceeding is lost. This is done in the knowledge that each hour of trial is worth $400 in fees and that sooner or later the judge will screw up and create some reasonable basis for an appeal, for which you can bill at least an additional $10,000.

malice aforethought. Premeditation of an illegitimate act, such as presenting arguments or facts not established as true to a tribunal under the guise of zealous representation.

malicious prosecution. Too many bleeding hearts and lazy slobs desperate for any job they can get become prosecuting attorneys and plea bargain every case that crosses their desk. The choice of prosecuting attorney might determine whether a rapist or murder will spend the rest of his life in jail or get out and cross my daughter's path a few years from now, so a good prosecutor is as ambitious as Satan and as mean as a snake.

malpractice insurance. The gravy train for trial lawyers.

manual labor. Something with which more lawyers should have personal experience.

marriage. Nobody knows what it means. A reliable definition should emerge in twenty-five to thirty years.

Mason, Perry. Pulp-fiction criminal defense lawyer created by writer Erle Stanley Gardener and brought to life on television by Raymond Burr. He provided innumerable examples of how *not* to cross-examine a witness.

Matlock, Ben. A fictional attorney apparently created by writers who never set foot in a courtroom, read a transcript, or consulted an attorney.

maundering. 1. Rambling, pointless speech. 2. Oral arguments.

***McCulloch v. Maryland,* 17 U. S. (4 Wheat.) 316 (1819).** The case in which the Supreme Court determined that the "necessary and proper" clause of the United States Constitution should have been "whatever Congress thinks is a good idea" clause.

McNaughton Rule. It is better to be insensible than insane.

mendacity. An essential quality of pleadings, briefs, and closing arguments.

mens rea. Latin for "guilty mind," derived from the natural state of the male psyche, particularly those who are married.

merely. An irresistible little insult to the arguments and intellect of opposing lawyers. Overuse has rendered this word meaningless. *See clearly.*

***Miller v. California,* 413 U.S. 15 (1973).** The case that made the United States the world leader in pornography.

Minnesota Twins, The. Warren Burger and Harry Blackmun, Chief Justice and Associate Justice of the United Sates Supreme Court, serving from 1969 to 1986 and 1970 to 1994, respectively.

monopoly. A monopoly exists when a single entity acts as the sole provider of a particular service, product, or commodity. The existence of monopolies in business is prohibited because they cause waste, inefficiency, price gouging, and corruption—and the government wishes to be the leader in these areas. (See, for example, public schools in New York City and Washington, D.C.)

mortgage insurance. An insurance policy that some lenders require borrowers to obtain. The borrower pays a monthly fee, and if the borrower defaults, the insurance company—which is probably owned by the lending institution—pays off the loan. This is a complete rip-off, considering the lower cost of good term life insurance, and considering that lenders retain the right to foreclose on the property and mark up their interest rates based on risk of default. Thus, the payments amount to thinly veiled extortion and the premium is fraudulently determined because it is not tied to the actual risk of financial loss for the sponsoring institution.

multistate. The first portion of the bar examination, used by several states to test bar applicants' knowledge of general legal principals. This portion of the test is as much a reading comprehension test as it is an examination of legal knowledge. After a long, contrived fact pattern suitable for a John Grisham novel, it asks a series of multiple choice questions. If the words "multiple choice" make you think "no problem," think again. The questions are usually something like this:

All of the following answers are wrong. Which is the least wrong?:

(A) Move to dismiss citing *People v. Rosario;*

(B) Move to suppress evidence citing *People v. Rosario;*

(C) Move for an Order to Produce citing *People v. Rosario;*

(D) Move to dismiss based on *Mapp v. Ohio.*

NIGGLE, BECKER, GRUDGE AND STAHL,
P.L.L.C.
INSURANCE DEFENSE

National Environmental Policy Act (N.E.P.A.), 42 U.S.C. 4321 et seq. A statute that requires agencies of the federal government to expend large amounts of time and money to determine the environmental effects of their actions and prepare environmental impact statements before doing what they damn well please anyway.

navigable waters. 1. *rational.* A body of water that may be used to convey vessels or materials from one location to another. 2. *modern.* Any semi-permanent surface water connected to a body of water that, in turn, may be used in commerce. *Refer to Rapanos v. United States, No. 04-1034 (2006).* Or, any lands contiguous to the navigable waters of the United States, whether or not those lands are inundated, provided they contain hydric soils and sustain plant species indicative of significant periods of soil saturation.

negligence. Contingency fees on the hoof.

New York. The center of the universe. Unless you make it there, you haven't made it.

New York lawyers. Creatures more vicious than rabid pit bull terriers.

N.I.M.B.Y. Abbreviation for Not In My Back Yard. The legislature, being filled with politicians who know nothing about science, math, or objective standards of any kind, have failed to put any objective measures stating what must be done to obtain approval for a project subjected to an environmental impact review. Therefore, anyone who opposes a project can kill it by hiring a lawyer with some expert to claim issues exist and then dragging out the process until the applicant decides it would be simpler to import its product from Mexico or China.

Ninth Amendment. This portion of the Bill of Rights states that the listing of certain rights in the Constitution did not deny the existence of other fundamental rights. However, the legal system being controlled by lawyers, and lawyers being concerned exclusively with precedent and black letter law, courts have all but ignored this provision. Conservative jurists in particular find this inconvenient as they argue against *Roe v. Wade* by saying that a right to privacy cannot be found in the Constitution.

no-knock warrant. "Ready or not, here we come!"

non-acquiescence. A doctrine by which federal agencies, such as the I.R.S., ignore judicial decisions that they don't like so they can continue screwing everyone who lacks the money or the courage to challenge the agency's abusive, arbitrary, or illegal practices in court.

nonprofit corporation. A corporation formed to avoid corporate tax liability and thus maximize the amount of corporate income available to pay executive salaries.

nutshell. A series of small books—*Torts in a Nutshell, Contracts in a Nutshell,* etc.—sold as study aids, similar to Cliff's Notes. These books attempt to state all the significant rules of an area of law as concisely as possible. The utility of these books is doubtful because they are primarily relied upon by people who failed to understand the law when it was fully explained to them.

OWEN, MOORE, TAN, ICHAN, PAY, & HOWE
ATTORNEYS AT LAW
YOUR BANKRUPTCY SPECIALISTS*

*CASH RETAINERS REQUIRED

obiter dictum. Desultory passages of judicial decisions in which judges reveal their opinion of themselves.

objection. An interjection used in court to interrupt the flow of an opposing counsel's examination of a witness, sometimes used to interrupt a witness and break his concentration, occasionally used to note for the record an exception to the ruling of a court, and at rare moments, used to stop a proceeding so the court can prevent irrelevant or impermissible evidence from entering the record.

obscenity. Any form of expression is obscene if, to the average person, applying contemporary community standards, the dominant theme of the material, taken as a whole, appeals to the prurient interest, is utterly without redeeming social importance, goes substantially beyond customary limits of candor in description or representation, is characterized by patent offensiveness, *and* is hardcore pornography. *Miller v. California,* 413 U.S. 15 (1973). *See pornography.* (You won't have to look too hard to find it.)

of counsel. A marketing gimmick in which a law firm places the name of a prominent attorney on the firm's letterhead even though that attorney doesn't actually work there.

offer. An attempt to take advantage of someone.

Old Bailey. Popular name of Central Criminal Court located on Bailey Street, London, not far from the former Newgate prison. Popularized internationally by the long-suffering fictitious barrister, Rumpole, and his wife—she who must be obeyed.

oligarchy. A system of government in which the majority leaders of both houses of the legislature, the governor, and the largest contributors to their respective campaigns control the governance of the state—e.g., New York State.

omnibus motion. In criminal proceedings, some jurisdictions require that all pretrial requests and motions be combined into a single motion made at a set length of time prior to the trial date, after which the defense can be expected to file at least another half-dozen pretrial motions.

on or about. A standard phrase used in affidavits and testimony to describe the date of an occurrence because "Oh hell, I can't remember" doesn't imply rectitude.

oral argument. A short oral recounting of the points already made to a court in writing on some matter of law regarding a motion or an appeal. Other than increasing the number of billable hours charged in a case, oral argument has little, if any, influence. Judges (or their clerks) will have read the papers and decided—long before you open your mouth—that you're wasting their time.

originalist. One who seeks to apply the law, particularly the United States Constitution, by channeling the spirits of the dead founding fathers and asking their opinions regarding the application of the law to present situations.

orphan case. A meritorious cause of action that no attorney will handle because it has little or no potential to result in an a monetary award that would fairly compensate for the time that would be necessary to prosecute the matter. To be worthwhile, one-third of the potential damages in a case (the lawyer's potential fee) must equal the number of hours needed to prosecute the case multiplied by a reasonable hourly fee, assuming the lawyer doesn't have trouble finding work. This sounds too much like algebra, and if most lawyers were good at math, they would have become engineers, doctors, or accountants. Rather than discipline themselves to learn ninth-grade math, lawyers have inflated damages so that a bruised toe is now "a serious contusion" worth $10,000,000 in damages.

PINE & HOWELL
ATTORNEYS AT LAW
DIVORCE,
CUSTODY,
PATERNITY, AND
PARENTAL RIGHTS

palimony. This court-mandated monetary compensation paid to paramours following the end of relationships converted live-in love interests to prostitutes who run a tab.

parole. The release of a felon from prison before he serves his entire sentence conditioned on his promise to behave himself. Because the criminal wouldn't have been in prison if he could follow rules and keep promises in the first place, and everyone agrees prison reinforces antisocial tendencies rather than rehabilitates them, it is a system based on foolish optimism.

paternity. 1. The physical fact of having issued the spermatozoon that fertilized an egg that resulted in the birth of a child. 2. A state of affairs that offers an opportunity for a man's life to have meaning.

paternity test. An odd form of test that determines whether one has in fact become a father. While virtually every other skilled or intellectual activity—from driving to practicing a profession—requires one to pass a test beforehand to prove qualification to undertake the pursuit, a paternity test is given only after the fact.

penultimate. One step short of the ultimate. Because we live in the culture of hyperbole, many people use penultimate to mean some kind of super-duper-hyper-extreme beyond ultimate thing. Nothing exists beyond the ultimate. Ultimate cannot be boosted by a modifier. The penultimate decision is the second-to-last decision; e.g., "The First Circuit Court of Appeals rendered the penultimate decision."

perspicuity. Having the attribute of being clearly stated and easily comprehended. This word frightens and insults attorneys and should not be used where they might hear it.

Pike **test.** A two-part inquiry pursuant to which federal judges determine whether state policies and the legislation implementing those policies are worthy of existence. *Refer to Pike v. Bruce Church, 397 U.S. 137 (1970).*

plea bargain. An economic microcosm in which criminals purchase lesser sentences from prosecutors by helping the prosecutor avoid work.

Plessy v. Ferguson. A case in which the United States Supreme Court exalted individual liberty by declaring that laws requiring African-Americans to occupy or use "separate but equal" facilities were constitutional. This case illustrates the infallible wisdom of Supreme Court Justices and the sacred nature of their decisions, which justifies blind adherence to the principle of *stare decisis.*

poach. To take clients away from other attorneys. The term is indicative of the client as a creature *ferae naturae*, but the term also reflects the concept that a prospective client is considered the possession of the attorney who first captures it.

P.O.P.O. Abbreviation for Pissed Off Police Officer. The term cannot be found in any penal code, but it is universally understood that pissing off the police officer is an aggravating factor that increases the severity of the consequences for any offense or crime.

pornography. Obscene literature or that which pertains to it.[3]

"potted plant, I'm not a." A pathetic plaintive plea to an insensitive inquisitor by an anxious attorney attempting to attain inclusion in an interrogation.

poverty law. A staple of practice for young lawyers starting out without a job at a major firm. Fortunately, young lawyers unable to find work in a significant firm are well qualified to practice in this field because of their intimate knowledge of poverty.

prenuptial agreement. A document in which lawyers use several hundred to several thousand words to say

---

[3] These circular definitions of obscenity and pornography came from an expensive, highly regarded law dictionary. It's funny, unless you were the student who spent fourteen hours working a minimum wage job to pay for it.

"darling, I don't trust you." Prenuptial agreements are frowned on by moral pro-family conservative people because they allow one party to continue screwing the other after the marital relationship ends.

prevarication. An advanced practical skill taught at most law schools. Lawyers especially skilled in this art often advance from law to politics.

product liability. From each according to his insurance limit to each according to his stupidity.

prior inconsistent statement. This is the blockbuster of cross-examination when properly executed. Unfortunately, most of the time, the supposed bomb is a dud. A witness could read a deposition transcript verbatim and the cross-examining lawyer, desperate for a Perry Mason moment, would claim the witness had contradicted herself.

prior restraint. A qualification on the resumé of an adult film actress.

prisoner's dilemma. This is the classic scenario in which the police have two suspects but can't prove their case without a confession. They take the suspects to separate rooms and tell them that the first to rat out his buddy gets a plea deal with a light sentence. Inevitably, one or both crack and confess—

usually casting most of the blame on the other. Dr. John Nash won a Nobel Prize for explaining with mathematics why the best choice for each prisoner is to assume his buddy will screw him. In the real world, the prisoners don't confess after running a mathematical model of the situation in their mind. They confess because they are self-serving jerks who don't give a damn about anyone but themselves and they know that their buddies are also self-serving jerks who will screw them in a heartbeat. That's why they are criminals.

professional responsibility. The body of law dealing with ethical obligations imposed on lawyers by states and bar associations. The bar adopted the term *professional responsibility* because lawyers were tired of hearing people tell them that the term *legal ethics* formed an oxymoron.

prolix. To be tediously long. This is one of the essential elements of successful legal writing, as exhaustive research and excruciating attention to minutiae generates billable hours that cannot be disputed. What client can rightly complain that their lawyer has been too thorough?

public interest law. Any field of law through which self-righteous zealots use the legal system to extort money from, and inflict misery on, productive members of society.

public interest lawyer. A product of the upper-middle-class who whines that someone else should pay off his student loans so he will be free to serve the proletarian revolution and bring about the workers' paradise.

punitive damages. Damages awarded because the jury believes the defendant is rich and got that way by screwing them.

debt • bait and switch • bankrupt • bankruptcy •bar •bar review course • basis • bench • best evidence rule • big gun •bilious •billable hour •birdie •black
ck letter law • blue book • bogart • bogie • boiler plate • bonus • book •boot •booty • bork •bribe • bust •busted • c.a.f.o. •calendar call • chain • child su
rning the file • circumstantial evidence •citation • class action • clearly • clients • closing costs • coffee • comparative negligence • compensatory damag
ideration • constitutional law • contract • contributory negligence • contumacious •corporation • corpus delicti • counselor • creditor • cross examination • dea
d man's acts • deceit • deep pocket • de minimis non curat lex • demurrer • deposition • derogatory clause • devil's dictionary • dictionary, law • directed
closure • divorce • dormant commerce clause • dorr's Rebellion • double billing • double jeopardy • due process • dying declaration • e.s o p. employee share ov
plan • eagle • economic development program • ego • eighth amendment •ejuration • entitlement • equal protection clause • equity • escheat •estate • est
pel, equitable • ethics • evidence, laws of / rules of • excited utterance • exclusionary rule • exculpatory evidence rule • exhaustion of remedies • ex-wif
and • face time • fair • fair use doctrine • fairway • false arrest • federal judge • federalism • federalism • federal witness protection program • federalist so
h amendment • fifteenth amendment • filibuster • first amendment • floating crap game • fourteenth amendment • fourth amendment • force majeure • frau
age •fraud • frivolous • fruit of the poisonous tree • fundamental right • garden • general denial • gerrymander • gift tax • gift tax • gloss • good sa
tatutes • got my papers! • great compromise • graft • gross • guarantee clause • guilt • h.a.p. • habeas corpus • habitability • habitability, warrantee of • ha
Learned • harmless error • harvard law • hassle • hazardous • hazardous waste • headnote • hearsay • heirloom • hereinabove, hereinafter, heretofore • he
aid • homicide • hornbook • hose • hundred weight • hung jury • ill fame • immoral • impediment to marriage • import-export clause • imputed negligence • imp
orporation by reference • income • inchoate • indemnity • indigent • inevitable discovery rule • infancy • internal Revenue code • internal Revenue service •
al property • interstate commerce • ipso facto • irrelevant • jack • jeopardy • judicial review • jump • jail • jailhouse lawyer • joint and several liability • journa
age • judgment • judgment not withstanding the verdict • jurisprudence • jury • jury instructions • jury wheel • just compensation • justice • justification • k
ver-cellars act • kentucky rule • kick • kickback • kilo • kiting • kleptomania • knock and announce • know • know-it-all • known-heirs • laches, estoppel by •
act • lapse in judgement • law • law of the case • law review • lawyer's trust account • lead counsel • legislative intent • liability • libel • link • liquidated dam
• loaded • long-arm jurisdiction • lose • maintenance • malice aforethought • malicious prosecution • malpractice insurance • manual labor • making a re
rriage • marrone • mason • matlock, ben • maundering • mcnaughton Rule • mendacity • mens rea • merely • minnesota twins, the • monopoly • mortgage i
• multi-state • navigable waters • negligence • new york • new york lawyers • ninth amendment • no-knock warrant • not-for-profit corporation • nutshell • c
n • objection • obscenity • offer • old bailey • oligarchy • originalist • paternity • paternity test • palimony • penultimate • perspicuity • pike test • plea ba
ssey v ferguson • potter, stewart • poverty law • pornography • prevarication • product liability • professional responsibility • prior inconsistent statement •
aint • profix • public interest law • public interest lawyer • punitive damages • quantum meruit • quash • quarter section • question presented • quid pro quo •
deed • rational basis test • rejection • remand • residuum • residuum rule • res ipsa loquitor • res judicata • respondent superior • responsible o
• rule against perpetuities • screw • screw-the-pooch • second amendment • sentence • separation of powers • settlement • seventh amendment • sinking fu
nth amendment • sixth amendment • slander • solicitation • spendthrift • stare decisis • stages of marriage • statute • statutes of frauds • street lawyer •
ruction • strict scrutiny • sub rosa • substantive due process • sudden heat of passion • summer associate • taylor law • take it upstairs • taxation • tenth am
• think-they-know-it-all • third amendment • tickle • title insurance • tort • to wit • traduce • trespass • trust • ultimate • unambiguous • unconstitutional • un
iercial code • unique • united states supreme court • unjust enrichment • usury • usufruct • vagrant • verified pleading • very • waiver • warhorse • warr
ss • warranty, implied • warranty period • ways-and-means • webster, daniel • west publishing • whole-life insurance • writ, william • withholding • yield •
el • zealous representation • zone of interest law • zoning • absence of malice • accessory • accomplice • acquit • act of god • action • activist judge • actus
ninistrative law • admiralty law • agent • albatross • alimony • alternative pleading • amnesty • ambulance chaser • antitrust laws • appeal • arbitrary and c
• armed and dangerous • as is • assumpsit • attorney • b.m w. • bad debt • bait and switch • bankrupt • bankruptcy •bar •bar review course • basis • ber
evidence rule • big gun •bilious •billable hour •birdie •black acre • black letter law • blue book • bogart • bogie • boiler plate • bonus • book •boot •booty
e • bust •busted • c.a.f.o. •calendar call • chain • child support •churning the file • circumstantial evidence •citation • class action • clearly • clients • cle
• coffee • comparative negligence • compensatorfy damages • consideration • constitutional law • contract • contributory negligence • contumacious •corp
• corpus delicti • counselor • creditor • cross examination • dead file • dead man's acts • deceit • deep pocket • de minimis non curat lex • demurrer • depos
ogatory clause • devil's dictionary • dictionary, law • directed verdict • disclosure • divorce • dormant commerce clause • dorr's Rebellion • double billing • do
rdy • due process • dying declaration • e.s.o.p. employee share ownership plan • eagle absence of malice • accessory • accomplice • acquit • act of god • a
ivist judge • actus reus • administrative law • admiralty law • agent • albatross • alimony • alternative pleading • amnesty • ambulance chaser • antitrust la
al • arbitrary and capricious • armed and dangerous • as is • assumpsit • attorney • b.m.w • bad debt • bait and switch • bankrupt • bankruptcy •bar •bar re
e • basis • bench • best evidence rule • big gun •bilious •billable hour •birdie •black acre • black letter law • blue book • bogart • bogie • boiler plate • bor
•boot •booty • bork •bribe • bust •busted • c.a f.o •calendar call • chain • child support •churning the file • circumstantial evidence •citation • class acti
y • clients • closing costs • coffee • comparative negligence • compensatory damages • consideration • constitutional law • contract • contributory negligen
macious •corporation • corpus delicti • counselor • creditor • cross examination • dead file • dead man's acts • deceit • deep pocket • de minimis non curat l
rrer • deposition • derogatory clause • devil's dictionary • dictionary, law • directed verdict • disclosure • divorce • dormant commerce clause • dorr's Rebell
e billing • double jeopardy • due process • dying declaration • e.s o p. employee share ownership plan • eagle • economic development program • ego • e
dment •ejuration • entitlement • equal protection clause • equity • escheat •estate • estop • estoppel, equitable • ethics • evidence, laws of / rules of • exi
ince • exclusionary rule • exculpatory evidence rule • exhaustion of remedies • ex-wife/ex-husband • face time • fair • fair use doctrine • fairway • false arre
al judge • federalism • federal witness protection program • federalist society • fifth amendment • filibuster • first amendment • floating crap game • fourte
dment • fourth amendment • force majeure • franking privilege •fraud • frivolous • fruit of the poisonous tree • fundamental right • garden • general denial • g
er • • gift causa mortis • gift tax • gluss • good samaritan statues • got my papers! • great compromise • graft • gross • guarantee clause • guilt • h.a.p. • ha
s • habitability • habitability, warrantee of • hack • hand, Learned • harmless error • harvard law • hassle • hazardous • hazardous waste • headnote • hears

QUIBBEL & BECKER
MEDIATION AND ARBITRATION

quantum meruit. Don't expect something for nothing.

quarter section. 160 acres, 25,600 square rods, 6,969,600 square feet, 1,003,622,400.0000002 square inches. The ease of such conversion is a natural reason for avoiding the more cumbersome metric system, in which 1 square kilometer is 100 hectares, 10,000 ares, or 1,000,000 square meters.

quash. The coolest word in the legal lexicon. Half the subpoenas issued have been challenged just to give a lawyer an excuse to say "quash."

question presented. The introductory section of an appellate brief in which a lawyer states all the essential facts and elements of the case in one interminable sentence ending with a question mark. For example:

When a legal writing professor has directed students to use short declarative sentences and to follow the guidance contained in the *Elements of Style* or *On Writing Well,* did the professor err in assigning a grade of "C" to a student who submitted a mock brief in response to a class assignment if the question presented in the student's brief contained more than one sentence? Brief Answer: Yes.

A real question presented might look something like this:

Did the federal district court err in holding that it lacked jurisdiction to hear challenges to the contents of an air pollution control permit issued by a state agency to an industrial facility when Article III of the United States Constitution restricts federal judicial jurisdiction to cases and controversies arising under federal law; the federal government has no permitting program or regulatory standards applicable to minor air contamination sources; and the state permit limits emissions from the facility so that the facility is a minor source of regulated air contaminants? Brief Answer: No.

Get all that the first time you read it? A judge wouldn't either. Questions presented are art like the poetry of Susan Sontag or the novels of James Joyce. Academics appreciate them, everyone lauds them, but nobody understands them.

quid pro quo. "I'll show you mine if you show me yours."

quitclaim deed. A document that conveys an unknown or uncertain interest in real property, such that the buyer cannot know what, if anything, (s)he is actually acquiring. The remarkable effect is that this document converts a potential fraud into a valid real estate transaction.

debt • bait and switch • bankrupt • bankruptcy •bar •bar review course • basis • bench • best evidence rule • big gun •bilious •billable hour •birdie •black

k letter law • blue book • bogart • bogie • boiler plate • bonus • book •boot •booty • bork •bribe • bust •busted • c.a.f.o. •calendar call • chain • child sup

hing the file • circumstantial evidence •citation • class action • clearly • clients • closing costs • coffee • comparative negligence • compensatory damage

leration • constitutional law • contract • contributory negligence • contumacious • corporation • corpus delicti • counselor • creditor • cross examination • dead

d man's acts • deceit • deep pocket • de minimis non curat lex • demurrer • deposition • derogatory clause • devil's dictionary • dictionary, law • directed ve

losure • divorce • dormant commerce clause • dorr's Rebellion • double billing • double jeopardy • due process • dying declaration • e.s.o.p. employee share ow

lan • eagle • economic development program • ego • eighth amendment •ejuration • entitlement • equal protection clause • equity • escheat •estate • est

el, equitable • ethics • evidence, laws of / rules of • excited utterance • exclusionary rule • exculpatory evidence rule • exhaustion of remedies • ex-wife

nd • face time • fair • fair use doctrine • fairway • false arrest • federal judge • federalism • federalism • federal witness protection program • federalist soc

amendment • fifteenth amendment • filibuster • first amendment • floating crap game • fourteenth amendment • fourth amendment • force majeure • fran

ge •fraud • frivolous • fruit of the poisonous tree • fundamental right • garden • general denial • gerrymander • gift causa mortis • gift tax • gloss • good sam

atues • got my papers! • great compromise • graft • gross • guarantee clause • guilt • h.a.p. • habeas corpus • habitability • habitability, warrantee of • ha

Learned • harmless error • harvard law • hassle • hazardous • hazardous waste • headnote • hearsay • heirloom • hereinabove, hereinafter, heretofore • he s

id • homicide • hornbook • hose • hundred weight • hung jury • ill fame • immoral • impediment to marriage • import-export clause • imputed negligence • impe

rporation by reference • income • inchoate • indemnity • indigent • inevitable discovery rule • infancy • internal Revenue code • internal Revenue service • ir

l property • interstate commerce • ipso facto • irrelevant • jack • jeopardy • judicial review • jump • jail • jailhouse lawyer • joint and several liability • journali

ge • judgment • judgment not withstanding the verdict • jurisprudence • jury • jury instructions • jury wheel • just compensation • justice • justification • k

ver-cellars act • kentucky rule • kick • kickback • kilo • kiting • kleptomania • knock and announce • know • know-it-all • known-heirs • laches, estoppel by

act • lapse in judgement • law • law of the case • law review • lawyer's trust account • lead counsel • legislative intent • liability • libel • link • liquidated dama

riage • marrone • mason • matlock, ben • maundering • mcnaughton Rule • mendacity • mens rea • merely • minnesota twins, the • monopoly • mortgage in

• multi-state • navigable waters • negligence • new york • new york lawyers • ninth amendment • no-knock warrant • not-for-profit corporation • nutshell • o

1 • objection • obscenity • offer • old bailey • oligarchy • originalist • paternity • paternity test • palimony • penultimate • perspicuity • pike test • plea bar

sey v. ferguson • potter, stewart • poverty law • pornography • prevarication • product liability • professional responsibility • prior inconsistent statement • r

nt • prolix • public interest law • public interest lawyer • punitive damages • quantum meruit • quash • quarter section • question presented • quid pro quo • e

deed • rainmaker • rational basis test • rejection • remand • residuum • residuum rule • res ipsa loquitor • res judicata • respondent superior • responsible off

rule against perpetuities • screw • screw-the-pooch • second amendment • sentence • separation of powers • settlement • seventh amendment • sinking fu

nth amendment • sixth amendment • slander • solicitation • spendthrift • stare decisis • stages of marriage • statute • statutes of frauds • street lawyer • st

uction • strict scrutiny • sub rosa • substantive due process • sudden heat of passion • summer associate • taylor law • take it upstairs • taxation • tenth ame

• think-they-know-it-all • third amendment • tickle • title insurance • tort • to wit • traduce • trespass • trust • ultimate • unambiguous • unconstitutional • unil

ercial code • unique • united states supreme court • unjust enrichment • usury • usufruct • vagrant • verified pleading • very • waiver • warhorse • warra

ss • warranty, implied • warranty period • ways-and-means • webster, daniel • west publishing • whole-life insurance • wirt, william • withholding • yield • y

al • zealous representation • zone of interest test • zoning • absence of malice • accessory • accomplice • acquit • act of god • action • activist judge • actus

inistrative law • admiralty law • agent • albatross • alimony • alternative pleading • amnesty • ambulance chaser • antitrust laws • appeal • arbitrary and ca

• armed and dangerous • as is • assumpsit • attorney • b.m.w. • bad debt • bait and switch • bankrupt • bankruptcy •bar •bar review course • basis • bene

vidence rule • big gun •bilious •billable hour •birdie •black acre • black letter law • blue book • bogart • bogie • boiler plate • bonus • book •boot •booty

e • bust •busted • c.a.f.o. •calendar call • chain • child support •churning the file • circumstantial evidence •citation • class action • clearly • clients • clo

• coffee • comparative negligence • compensatoFy damages • consideration • constitutional law • contract • contributory negligence • contumacious •corp

corpus delicti • counselor • creditor • cross examination • dead file • dead man's acts • deceit • deep pocket • de minimis non curat lex • demurrer • depos

gatory clause • devil's dictionary • dictionary, law • directed verdict • disclosure • divorce • dormant commerce clause • dorr's Rebellion • double billing • do

rdy • due process • dying declaration • e.s.o.p. employee share ownership plan • eagle absence of malice • accessory • accomplice • acquit • act of god • ac

vist judge • actus reus • administrative law • admiralty law • agent • albatross • alimony • alternative pleading • amnesty • ambulance chaser • antitrust law

l • arbitrary and capricious • armed and dangerous • as is • assumpsit • attorney • b.m.w. • bad debt • bait and switch • bankrupt • bankruptcy •bar •bar rev

e • basis • bench • best evidence rule • big gun •bilious •billable hour •birdie •black acre • black letter law • blue book • bogart • bogie • boiler plate • bon

•boot •booty • bork •bribe • bust •busted • c.a.t.o. •calendar call • chain • child support •churning the file • circumstantial evidence •citation • class actio

y • clients • closing costs • coffee • comparative negligence • compensatory damages • consideration • constitutional law • contract • contributory negligen

macious •corporation • corpus delicti • counselor • creditor • cross examination • dead file • dead man's acts • deceit • deep pocket • de minimis non curat

rrer • deposition • derogatory clause • devil's dictionary • dictionary, law • directed verdict • disclosure • divorce • dormant commerce clause • dorr's Rebelli

e billing • double jeopardy • due process • dying declaration • e.s.o.p. employee share ownership plan • eagle • economic development program • ego • ei

dment •ejuration • entitlement • equal protection clause • equity • escheat •estate • estop • estoppel, equitable • ethics • evidence, laws of / rules of • exc

nce • exclusionary rule • exculpatory evidence rule • exhaustion of remedies • ex-wife/ex-husband • face time • fair • fair use doctrine • fairway • false arre

al judge • federalism • federal witness protection program • federalist society • fifth amendment • filibuster • first amendment • floating crap game • fourte

dment • fourth amendment • force majeure • franking privilege •fraud • frivolous • fruit of the poisonous tree • fundamental right • garden • general denial • ge

s • gift causa mortis • gift tax • gloss • good samaritan statues • got my papers! • great compromise • graft • gross • guarantee clause • guilt • h a p. • hab

s • habitability • habitability, warrantee of • hack • hand, Learned • harmless error • harvard law • hassle • hazardous • hazardous waste • headnote • hears

RAINE, HALE, SNOW AND EISS
ATTORNEYS AT LAW
F.E.M.A. APPLICATIONS
INSURANCE CLAIMS
CROP DAMAGE &
PERFORMANCE DISPUTES

rainmaker. A lawyer who might be a blithering idiot, but who brings well-heeled clients and lucrative business to a firm.

rational basis test. The doctrine that a court will not substitute its judgment for that of a legislative or administrative body if that body had a rational basis to take the action being reviewed by the court. This presumes that one can rely on a judge to comprehend what may or may not be rational.

rejection. The moment when one of the parties to a negotiation comes to his senses.

remand. An appellate court's direction returning a case to a lower court for further proceedings from which additional appeals may be taken, resulting in subsequent remand for further proceedings, until one or both parties become unwilling to—or incapable of—paying additional legal fees.

residuum. The amount of a judgment or award delivered to a client after deduction of legal fees and expenses.

residuum rule. An outdated doctrine that required the decision of an administrative proceeding to be based on at least a residuum of competent evidence.

res ipsa loquitor. Latin for "Duh."

res judicata. Latin for "You lost, get over it."

respondent superior. Latin for "Sue the one with the most money."

responsible officer rule. A principle of empowerment through which shareholders, directors, and executives blame corporate wrongdoing on the lowliest employee connected to an unlawful activity.

Rowan v. Runnels, **46 U.S. (5 How.) 134 (1847).** The case in which the United States Supreme Court determined that its prior fact-specific holdings regarding application of a state's law were in fact a general law of the United States superceding all state law.

rule against perpetuities. An interest in real property must vest, if at all, within twenty-one years and nine months of the termination of a life that is in being at the time of the creation of the interest. If you have a hard time understanding this, don't worry too much. You and your client will probably be dead before anyone notices you've committed malpractice.

debt • bait and switch • bankrupt • bankruptcy • bar • bar review course • basis • bench • best evidence rule • big gun •bilious •billable hour •birdie •black
ck letter law • blue book • bogart • bogie • boiler plate • bonus • book • boot • booty • bork • bribe • bust • busted • c.a.f.o. • calendar call • chain • child sup
ning the file • circumstantial evidence •citation • class action • clearly • clients • closing costs • coffee • comparative negligence • compensatory damage
deration • constitutional law • contract • contributory negligence • contumacious •corporation • corpus delicti • counselor • creditor • cross examination • dead
d man's acts • deceit • deep pocket • de minimis non curat lex • demurrer • deposition • derogatory clause • devil's dictionary • dictionary, law • directed ve
losure • divorce • dormant commerce clause • dorr's Rebellion • double billing • double jeopardy • due process • dying declaration • e.s.o.p. employee share ow
alan • eagle • economic development program • ego • eighth amendment • ejuration • entitlement • equal protection clause • equity • escheat •estate • esto
pel, equitable • ethics • evidence, laws of / rules of • excited utterance • exclusionary rule • exculpatory evidence rule • exhaustion of remedies • ex-wife
nd • face time • fair • fair use doctrine • fairway • false arrest • federal judge • federalism • federalism • federal witness protection program • federalist soc
amendment • fifteenth amendment • filibuster • first amendment • floating crap game • fourteenth amendment • fourth amendment • force majeure • fran
ge • fraud • frivolous • fruit of the poisonous tree • fundamental right • garden • general denial • gerrymander • gift causa mortis • gift tax • gloss • good sa
tatues • got my papers! • great compromise • graft • gross • guarantee clause • guilt • h.a.p. • habeas corpus • habitability • habitability, warrantee of • ha
Learned • harmless error • harvard law • hassle • hazardous • hazardous waste • headnote • hearsay • heirloom • hereinabove, hereinafter, heretofore • he s
aid • homicide • hornbook • hose • hundred weight • hung jury • ill fame • immoral • impediment to marriage • import-export clause • imputed negligence • impo
rporation by reference • income • inchoate • indemnity • indigent • inevitable discovery rule • infancy • internal Revenue code • internal Revenue service • in
al property • interstate commerce • ipso facto • irrelevant • jack • jeopardy • judicial review • jump • jail • jailhouse lawyer • joint and several liability • journal
ege • judgment • judgment not withstanding the verdict • jurisprudence • jury • jury instructions • jury wheel • just compensation • justice • justification • k
ver-legis act • kentucky law • kick • kickback • kilo • kiting • kleptomania • knock and announce • know • know-it-all • known-heirs • laches, estoppel by • l
act • lapse in judgement • law • law of the case • law review • lawyer's trust account • lead counsel • legislative intent • liability • libel • link • liquidated dama
ation • loaded • long-arm jurisdiction • lose • maintenance • malice aforethought • malicious prosecution • malpractice insurance • manual labor • making a re
riage • marrone • mason • matlock, ben • maundering • mcnaughton Rule • mendacity • mens rea • merely • minnesota twins, the • monopoly • mortgage in
• multi-state • navigable waters • negligence • new york • new york lawyers • ninth amendment • no-knock warrant • not-for-profit corporation • nutshell • ob
n • objection • obscenity • offer • old bailey • oligarchy • originalist • paternity • paternity test • palimony • penultimate • perspicuity • pike test • plea bar
ssey v. ferguson • potter, stewart • poverty law • pornography • prevarication • product liability • professional responsibility • prior inconsistent statement •
int • prolix • public interest law • public interest lawyer • punitive damages • quantum meruit • quash • quarter section • question presented • quid pro quo • q
deed • rainmaker • rational basis test • rejection • remand • residuum • residuum rule • res ipsa loquitor • res judicata • respondent superior • responsible off
rule against perpetuities • screw • screw-the-pooch • second amendment • sentence • separation of powers • settlement • seventh amendment • sinking fu
nth amendment • sixth amendment • slander • solicitation • spendthrift • stare decisis • stages of marriage • statute • statutes of frauds • street lawyer • s
uction • strict scrutiny • sub rosa • substantive due process • sudden heat of passion • summer associate • taylor law • take it upstairs • taxation • tenth am
• think-they-know-it-all • third amendment • tickle • title insurance • tort • to wit • traduce • trespass • trust • ultimate • unambiguous • unconstitutional • unif
ercial code • unique • united states supreme court • unjust enrichment • usury • usufruct • vagrant • verified pleading • very • waiver • warhorse • warra
ss • warranty, implied • warranty period • ways-and-means • webster, daniel • west publishing • whole-life insurance • wirt, william • withholding • yield • y
el • zealous representation • zone of interest test • zoning • absence of malice • accessory • accomplice • acquit • act of god • action • activist judge • actus r
inistrative law • admiralty law • agent • albatross • alimony • alternative pleading • amnesty • ambulance chaser • antitrust laws • appeal • arbitrary and ca
• armed and dangerous • as is • assumpsit • attorney • b.m.w. • bad debt • bait and switch • bankrupt • bankruptcy •bar •bar review course • basis • bene
vidence rule • big gun •bilious •billable hour •birdie •black acre • black letter law • blue book • bogart • bogie • boiler plate • bonus • book •boot •booty • b
e • bust •busted • c.a.f.o. •calendar call • chain • child support •churning the file • circumstantial evidence •citation • class action • clearly • clients • clo
• coffee • comparative negligence • compensatorfy damages • consideration • constitutional law • contract • contributory negligence • contumacious •corp
corpus delicti • counselor • creditor • cross examination • dead file • dead man's acts • deceit • deep pocket • de minimis non curat lex • demurrer • depos
gatory clause • devil's dictionary • dictionary, law • directed verdict • disclosure • divorce • dormant commerce clause • dorr's Rebellion • double billing • do
dy • due process • dying declaration • e.s.o.p. employee share ownership plan • eagle absence of malice • accessory • accomplice • acquit • act of god • ac
vist judge • actus reus • administrative law • admiralty law • agent • albatross • alimony • alternative pleading • amnesty • ambulance chaser • antitrust law
l • arbitrary and capricious • armed and dangerous • as is • assumpsit • attorney • b.m.w • bad debt • bait and switch • bankrupt • bankruptcy •bar •bar rev
• basis • bench • best evidence rule • big gun •bilious •billable hour •birdie •black acre • black letter law • blue book • bogart • bogie • boiler plate • bon
boot •booty • bork •bribe • bust •busted • c.a.f.o. •calendar call • chain • child support •churning the file • circumstantial evidence •citation • class actio
y • clients • closing costs • coffee • comparative negligence • compensatory damages • consideration • constitutional law • contract • contributory negligence
nacious •corporation • corpus delicti • counselor • creditor • cross examination • dead file • dead man's acts • deceit • deep pocket • de minimis non curat le
rrer • deposition • derogatory clause • devil's dictionary • dictionary, law • directed verdict • disclosure • divorce • dormant commerce clause • dorr's Rebelli
e billing • double jeopardy • due process • dying declaration • e.s.o.p. employee share ownership plan • eagle • economic development program • ego • ei
dment • ejuration • entitlement • equal protection clause • equity • escheat •estate • estop • estoppel, equitable • ethics • evidence, laws of / rules of • exc
nce • exclusionary rule • exculpatory evidence rule • exhaustion of remedies • ex-wife/ex-husband • face time • fair • fair use doctrine • fairway • false arre
al judge • federalism • federal witness protection program • federalist society • fifth amendment • filibuster • first amendment • floating crap game • fourtee
dment • fourth amendment • force majeure • franking privilege •fraud • frivolous • fruit of the poisonous tree • fundamental right • garden • general denial • g
er • gift causa mortis • gift tax • gloss • good samaritan statues • got my papers! • great compromise • graft • gross • guarantee clause • guilt • h.a.p. • hat
s • habitability, habitability, warrantee of • hack • hand, Learned • harmless error • harvard law • hassle • hazardous • hazardous waste • headnote • hearsa

SMALL AND PETTY
ATTORNEYS AT LAW
DIVORCE
CHILD CUSTODY
CHILD SUPPORT
ALIMONY—PALIMONY
PRENUPTIAL AGREEMENTS

said. Used as in " . . . said weapon . . ." Try using the word "the."

***Scott v. Sandford,* 60 U.S. 393 (1857).** Landmark United States Supreme Court decision highlighting the importance of allowing the justices to set national political policy. This decision has the additional benefit of illustrating the sacred nature of *stare decisis. See also Plessy v. Ferguson.*

screw. 1. To achieve an advantage for oneself at the expense of another, particularly through deceptive or secret actions. 2. What senior partners do with good-looking young associates during the annual holiday party. 3. What senior partners do to the other young associates the rest of the year.

screw the pooch. To lose a conflict or fail to achieve an objective through obvious or calamitous error. E.g., "You filed the complaint the day after the statute of limitations expired? Man, you really screwed the pooch."

Second Amendment. A dangerous historical anachronism that, thankfully, modern judges have practically excised from the Bill of Rights because they recognize that no individual has a legitimate purpose for a firearm.

sentence. 1. A noun and verb (subject and predicate) placed together to express a complete thought, around which lawyers hang numerous superfluous sesquipedalian words intended to convey their intellectual stature to the reader. 2. To pronounce the terms of punishment upon one who has been convicted of a crime. This was traditionally the purview of the judges who heard the cases. But meting out punishment seemed so gratifying that politicians, particularly Congress, couldn't resist taking over the job. *See sentencing guidelines.*

sentencing guidelines. 1. *The Elements of Style* by Strunk & White. 2. A matrix of factors that Congress has mandated federal judges use to ensure that criminals face the maximum sentences allowed by law.

separation of powers. The supposed division of the function and powers of government among the executive, legislative, and judicial branches of government. This inefficient and antiquated system has been replaced and all governmental functions have been placed in the hands of dedicated bureaucrats who are less apt than elected officials to be swayed by the vagaries of the ignorant masses.

settlement. Mutual capitulation.

Seventh Amendment. This Amendment to the United States Constitution guarantees the right to a jury trial in suits at common law where the value in controversy exceeds twenty dollars. This proved inconvenient when African-Americans sued to assert their right to freedom from slavery, so the courts decided to ignore it. *Refer to Miller v. McQuerry, 17 Fed Cas. 335 (1853).*

***Shelley's Case,* 76 Eng. Rep. (C.B. 1579).** If a grantor conveys a life estate to a grantee and in the same instrument conveys a contingent remainder to the grantee's heirs, the life estate merges with the remainder and the grantee obtains title in fee. This rule was intended to prevent tax evasion in feudal England. In a stunning demonstration of the progressive nature of common law courts, most American jurisdictions abolished the rule in the late twentieth century. Law professors pining for the 60s (the 1660s) continue to teach this pointless anachronism.

sinking fund. 1. The financial accounts of anyone with children. 2. Self-insurance for a boat.

Sixteenth Amendment. The death warrant for limited government.

Sixth Amendment. This Amendment to the United States Constitution is jam-packed with good stuff. It has effectively created a great criminal justice system with impartial juries; the right to know what the hell the government says you did; the right to an attorney; and, the right to subpoena and examine witnesses. It also promises a speedy trial, but what lawyers call "speedy" is what other people call forever-and-a-day. Still, four out of five isn't bad.

slander. The standard mode of political speech in America, particularly against the president, who—being a public figure—cannot seek redress. *See absence of malice.*

solicitation. 1. The practice in which lawyers pay other professionals to refer clients to them. This is similar to paying kickbacks except that the lawyers generally pay a flat fee rather than a percentage. 2. An offer to enter into a contract for the provision of sexual services other than those associated with production of a sexually explicit movie—which are inexplicably outside the scope of statutes that otherwise prohibit flesh peddling.

spendthrift. One who wastes money on items of little lasting value. E.g., any member of the United States Congress.

stages of marriage. Matrimony, acrimony, alimony.

stare decisis. Latin for "Being a United States Supreme Court justice means never having to say you're sorry."

statute. A positive law created by the legislature. In contrast with common law, the strictures of a statute are prospective and generally apply to an entire class of people or situations rather than particular parties sought to be regulated by the majority of politicians of the enacting body. This is rarely a good thing, because politicians almost never comprehend the ramifications of what they do on future situations.

statute of frauds. Law prohibiting the courts from enforcing oral contracts for designated classes of transactions. The statute was probably conceived because politicians were grossed out by glad-handing people who solemnized their bargains by spitting in their palms and then shaking hands.

statute of limitations. Abbreviated S.O.L. for good reason.

Stewart, Potter. He knew it when he saw it.

strategic lawsuit against public participation (S.L.A.P.P.). A lawsuit, usually asserting defamation or a related tort, initiated to intimidate opponents of a project or activity from expressing their views. University of Denver professors Penelope Canan and George W. Pring coined the apt acronym SLAPP. Some jurisdictions have passed anti-SLAPP statutes. However, the legislatures were concerned about denying people the right to sue if they really were defamed, and therefore most anti-SLAPP statutes are weak and require protracted litigation to enforce. Because SLAPP suits are usually filed by businesses who have bushels of cash and a pack of ravenous lawyers on retainer, and the defendants are individuals without much excess income to spend on lawyers, anti-SLAPP statutes are a bit like handing grandma a pea-shooter and asking her to stave off a company of Marines.

street lawyer. 1. A lawyer too stupid, inept, or lazy to obtain employment in a top East Coast law firm. 2. A lawyer who fails to make partner at a top firm. The term derives from the poor slobs who have to find clients "on the street."

strict construction. The application of positive law exactly as it is written using the most commonly accepted meanings of the words contained in the provision at issue. This fails to accept the reality that no two lawyers will ever agree about so much as the color of newly fallen snow.

strict scrutiny. A rigorous sounding—but wholly subjective—standard that a statute that infringes fundamental individual rights must withstand to be considered valid. *See fundamental rights.*

sub rosa. We could tell you the definition, but then we'd have to kill you.

substantive due process. A doctrine through which the justices of the United States Supreme Court invalidate laws they do not like even though they cannot find any conflict between the law and the Constitution. Chief Justice Roger Taney first used it to justify his claim that the Missouri Compromise was invalid and that Congress could not prohibit slavery. *See Scott v. Sandford.* Justices resurrected this idea after the Civil War to invalidate health, safety, and economic legislation. Shockingly, modern judges otherwise obsessed with stare decisis omit citations to *Scott v. Sandford* from their substantive due process decisions.

sudden heat of passion. A state of diminished mental capacity caused by extreme emotional disturbance. In law, this mitigates culpability for homicide, resulting in a charge or conviction for manslaughter rather than intentional murder. In real life, it is an aggravating factor in determining your spouse's reaction to any marital indiscretion.

summer associate. A law student engaged in an eight- to ten-week interview for a post-graduation job.

***Swift v. Tyson,* 41 U.S. (16 Pet.) 1 (1842).** Congress enacted Section 34 of the Judiciary Act of September 24, 1789, stating: "The laws of the several States . . . shall be regarded as rules of decision in trials at common law, in the courts of the United States, in cases where they apply. . ." Ignoring Congress, 1,000 years of British legal heritage, and the word "law" in common law, the Supreme Court decided that state common law was "at most only evidence of what the laws are, and are not themselves law . . ." Therefore, federal courts could do as they damn well pleased. *See Erie Railroad v. Tompkins, 304 U.S. 64 (1938).*

125

debt • bait and switch • bankrupt • bankruptcy • bar • bar review course • basis • bench • best evidence rule • big gun • bilious • billable hour • birdie • black
k letter law • blue book • bogart • bogie • boiler plate • bonus • book • boot • booty • bork • bribe • bust • busted • c.a.f.o. • calendar call • chain • child sup
ning the file • circumstantial evidence • citation • class action • clearly • clients • closing costs • coffee • comparative negligence • compensatory damag
feration • constitutional law • contract • contributory negligence • contumacious • corporation • corpus delicti • counselor • creditor • cross examination • dea
d man's acts • deceit • deep pocket • de minimis non curat lex • demurrer • deposition • derogatory clause • devil's dictionary • dictionary, law • directed ver
losure • divorce • dormant commerce clause • dorr's Rebellion • double billing • double jeopardy • due process • dying declaration • e.s.o.p. employee share ow
lan • eagle • economic development program • ego • eighth amendment • ejuration • entitlement • equal protection clause • equity • escheat • estate • est
pel, equitable • ethics • evidence, laws of / rules of • excited utterance • exclusionary rule • exculpatory evidence rule • exhaustion of remedies • ex-wife
nd • face time • fair • fair use doctrine • fairway • false arrest • federal judge • federalism • federalism • federal witness protection program • federalist so
• amendment • fifteenth amendment • filibuster • first amendment • floating crap game • fourteenth amendment • fourth amendment • force majeure • fran
ge • fraud • frivolous • fruit of the poisonous tree • fundamental right • garden • general denial • gerrymander • gift causa mortis • gift tax • gloss • good sa
tatues • got my papers! • great compromise • graft • gross • guarantee clause • guilt • h.a.p. • habeas corpus • habitability • habitability, warrantee of • ha
Learned • harmless error • harvard law • hassle • hazardous • hazardous waste • headnote • hearsay • heirloom • hereinabove, hereinafter, heretofore • he
aid • homicide • hornbook • hose • hundred weight • hung jury • ill fame • immoral • impediment to marriage • import-export clause • imputed negligence • imp
rporation by reference • income • inchoate • indemnity • indigent • inevitable discovery rule • infancy • internal Revenue code • internal Revenue service • i
al property • interstate commerce • ipso facto • irrelevant • jack • jeopardy • judicial review • jump • jail • jailhouse lawyer • joint and several liability • journa
ge • judgment • judgment notwithstanding the verdict • jurisprudence • jury • jury instructions • jury wheel • just compensation • justice • justification • k
wel-cellars act • kentucky rule • kick • kickback • kilo • kiting • kleptomania • knock and announce • know • know-it-all • known-heirs • laches, estoppel by •
act • lapse in judgement • law • law of the case • law review • lawyer's trust account • lead counsel • legislative intent • liability • libel • link • liquidated dam
ation • loaded • long-arm jurisdiction • lose • maintenance • malice aforethought • malicious prosecution • malpractice insurance • manual labor • making a re
riage • marrone • mason • matlock, ben • maundering • mcnaughton Rule • mendacity • mens rea • merely • minnesota twins, the • monopoly • mortgage i
• multi-state • navigable waters • negligence • new york • new york lawyers • ninth amendment • no-knock warrant • not-for-profit corporation • nutshell • o
in • objection • obscenity • offer • old bailey • oligarchy • originalist • paternity • paternity test • palimony • penultimate • perspicuity • pike test • plea bar
ssey v. ferguson • potter, stewart • poverty law • pomography • prevarication • product liability • professional responsibility • prior inconsistent statement • i
nt • prolix • public interest law • public interest lawyer • punitive damages • quantum meruit • quash • quarter section • question presented • quid pro quo •
deed • rainmaker • rational basis test • rejection • remand • residuum • residuum rule • res ipsa loquitor • res judicata • respondent superior • responsible of
rule against perpetuities • screw • screw-the-pooch • second amendment • sentence • separation of powers • settlement • seventh amendment • sinking fu
nth amendment • sixth amendment • slander • solicitation • spendthrift • stare decisis • stages of marriage • statute • statutes of frauds • street lawyer •
uction • strict scrutiny • sub rosa • substantive due process • sudden heat of passion • summer associate • taylor law • take it upstairs • taxation • tenth am
• think-they-know-it-all • third amendment • tickle • title insurance • tort • to wit • traduce • trespass • trust • ultimate • unambiguous • unconstitutional • unr
ercial code • unique • united states supreme court • unjust enrichment • usury • usufruct • vagrant • verified pleading • very • waiver • warhorse • warra
ss • warranty, implied • warranty period • ways-and-means • webster, daniel • west publishing • whole-life insurance • wirt, william • withholding • yield •
el • zealous representation • zone of interest test • zoning • absence of malice • accessory • accomplice • acquit • act of god • action • activist judge • actus
ninistrative law • admiralty law • agent • albatross • alimony • alternative pleading • amnesty • ambulance chaser • antitrust laws • appeal • arbitrary and c
• armed and dangerous • as is • assumpsit • attorney • b.m.w. • bad debt • bait and switch • bankrupt • bankruptcy • bar • bar review course • basis • ben
vidence rule • big gun • bilious • billable hour • birdie • black acre • black letter law • blue book • bogart • bogie • boiler plate • bonus • book • boot • booty •
e • bust • busted • c.a.f.o. • calendar call • chain • child support • churning the file • circumstantial evidence • citation • class action • clearly • clients • clo
• coffee • comparative negligence • compensatorFy damages • consideration • constitutional law • contract • contributory negligence • contumacious • corp
corpus delicti • counselor • creditor • cross examination • dead file • dead man's acts • deceit • deep pocket • de minimis non curat lex • demurrer • deposi
ogatory clause • devil's dictionary • dictionary, law • directed verdict • disclosure • divorce • dormant commerce clause • dorr's Rebellion • double billing • do
dy • due process • dying declaration • e.s.o.p. employee share ownership plan • eagle absence of malice • accessory • accomplice • acquit • act of god • ar
vist judge • actus reus • administrative law • admiralty law • agent • albatross • alimony • alternative pleading • amnesty • ambulance chaser • antitrust law
al • arbitrary and capricious • armed and dangerous • as is • assumpsit • attorney • b.m.w. • bad debt • bait and switch • bankrupt • bankruptcy • bar • bar re
e • basis • bench • best evidence rule • big gun • bilious • billable hour • birdie • black acre • black letter law • blue book • bogart • bogie • boiler plate • bon
boot • booty • bork • bribe • bust • busted • c.a.f.o. • calendar call • chain • child support • churning the file • circumstantial evidence • citation • class acti
• clients • closing costs • coffee • comparative negligence • compensatory damages • consideration • constitutional law • contract • contributory negligen
macious • corporation • corpus delicti • counselor • creditor • cross examination • dead file • dead man's acts • deceit • deep pocket • de minimis non curat l
rrer • deposition • derogatory clause • devil's dictionary • dictionary, law • directed verdict • disclosure • divorce • dormant commerce clause • dorr's Rebelli
e billing • double jeopardy • due process • dying declaration • e.s.o.p. employee share ownership plan • eagle • economic development program • ego • ei
dment • ejuration • entitlement • equal protection clause • equity • escheat • estate • estop • estoppel, equitable • ethics • evidence, laws of / rules of • exc
ance • exclusionary rule • exculpatory evidence rule • exhaustion of remedies • ex-wife/ex-husband • face time • fair • fair use doctrine • fairway • false arre
al judge • federalism • federal witness protection program • federalist society • fifth amendment • filibuster • first amendment • floating crap game • fourte
dment • fourth amendment • force majeure • franking privilege • fraud • frivolous • fruit of the poisonous tree • fundamental right • garden • general denial • ge
er • gift causa mortis • gift tax • gloss • good samaritan statues • got my papers! • great compromise • graft • gross • guarantee clause • guilt • h.a.p. • ha
s • habitability • habitability, warrantee of • hack • hand, Learned • harmless error • harvard law • hassle • hazardous • hazardous waste • headnote • hears
• hereinabove, hereinafter, heretofore • he said, she said • homicide • hornbook • hose • hundred weight • hung jury • ill fame • immoral • impedime

TRIPP AND SOO, A LAW FIRM
PERSONAL INJURY—PRODUCT LIABILITY
CLASS ACTION—EMOTIONAL DISTRESS

Taft, William Howard. A politician reputed by intellectuals and historians to be inept. His ineptitude is clear from his dearth of accomplishments. He did very little other than serve as Solicitor General of the United States, a federal judge, Governor-General of the Philippines, Secretary of War, President of the United States, professor of law at Yale, and Chief Justice of the United States.

take it upstairs. Manhattan slang for taking an appeal, originating from the location of the Second Circuit Court of Appeals "upstairs" from the Federal District courts for the Southern District of New York.

Taney, Roger B. This sickly son of slave-owning Maryland planters served as United States Attorney General and Secretary of the Treasury under Andrew Jackson. He ended the practice of depositing all of the receipts of the United States Treasury in a single privately run bank (owned by Daniel Webster's law clients and political patrons). When that bank collapsed in an embezzlement scandal, Taney appeared to be destined to take a place in history beside Alexander Hamilton. Instead, he became Chief Justice of the United States and is remembered for one sentence: "They [African-Americans] have no rights that a white man is bound to respect."

taxation. 1. A routine confiscation of money by government. 2. The power to destroy.

tax law. Physicist R.J.E. Clausius did not have legislation in mind when he observed that the universe experiences a perpetual increase in disorder. However, this is the only explanation for the Internal Revenue Code. There will probably never be an unemployed tax lawyer, but tax law is not for everyone. You have the potential to be a tax lawyer if you do the entire *New York Times* crossword puzzle in ink; you read the Old Testament, Joyce's *Ulysses*, or Tolkien's *Silmarilion* for pleasure; and, spend idle moments doing algebraic word problems.

Taylor law. A statute that prohibits public employees from striking, in return for which the government agrees employees will only be fired for cause— "'cause you screwed up," " 'cause we don't like you," " 'cause the governor promised to cut taxes without reducing spending on infrastructure, education, or social welfare," "'cause the senator's cousin's brother-in-law wants your job," and so forth.

Ten Commandments. An ancient set of laws reputedly handed down to Moses from God at the burning bush on Mount Sinai, a representation of which appears in the iconography of the Supreme Court of the United States as a symbol of the codification of law as a basis

129

for civil society. This symbolism is a sophisticated concept that the addled masses of Americans cannot grasp, and therefore representations of the Commandments on any public property other than the Supreme Court is an establishment of religion in violation of the prohibition of the First Amendment.

Tenth Amendment. This Amendment to the United States Constitution reserves for the states and the people all powers not explicitly delegated to the federal government. However, the expansive application of the powers to tax and spend (or not spend) and regulate commerce have rendered this provision meaningless except for historical context.

tenurial title. Real property held through grant of title originating with and at the sufferance of the sovereign. The United States continued this system after the Revolution, with most states passing laws divesting the king and anyone loyal to him of their title to land and vesting it in themselves. (These lands were then sold to pay for the war. That's the American way.) So, when the value of your house or business exceeds the cost of the bribes needed to convince your local politicians to condemn your property, they'll throw you out on your ass and give it to the developer with the most grease for their palms.

term of art. A mystical word or phrase that symbolizes an esoteric legal concept so that only those initiated in the secret society of lawyers can understand legal documents and proceedings.

think-they-know-it-all. Persons who—despite their ignorance—carry on as if they know more about everything than anyone else.

Third Amendment. This Amendment of the United States Constitution prohibits the quartering of soldiers in private homes and is one of the few Amendments that the Supreme Court has not had the chance to "interpret." Not that the federal government hasn't put soldiers in people's homes. During times of national crisis, citizens exhibit an inexplicable tendency to help the nation survive by helping our soldiers in any way they can rather than using the legal system as a self-destruct mechanism.

tickle. 1. To check someone's progress on a task. 2. A way to pass the buck and make your boss think you are working on a project when you haven't the foggiest idea what is happening with it. E.g., "I asked Perkins for a rundown on some case law. I'll plan on tickling him on that in a couple days."

title insurance. A conspiracy between banks and insurance companies in which the bank requires a borrower who is purchasing real property via a warranty deed to obtain an abstract of title, pay a lawyer to handle the transaction, and then pay outrageous sums of money for a policy that will satisfy the mortgage if a defect in title is found after the transaction is completed.

tort. Unrealized income for trial lawyers.

to wit. These words signal readers that the writer is wrapping up a rambling run-on sentence and is about to get to the point. E.g., "The defendant, Fanny Gigliotti, with a culpable mental state as defined in section 10 of the State of Decay Penal Code, on or about 1 July, 2007, at approximately 11:00 o'clock in the forenoon, did violate sections 140 and 145 of the Penal Law of the State of Decay by engaging in public the display of a person, *to wit:* starting a beach volleyball game in a thong bikini that failed to complete the game with her."

traduce. 1. To speak badly of or lie about someone with intent to expose them to ridicule. 2. As in cross-examination.

transition. 1. Provisions of a statute or regulation that tell people who spent huge amounts of money and organized their lives to comply with the law as it previously existed that they have to spend even more money and reorganize their lives because government changed its mind. 2. The period of time allotted to an outgoing executive—such as a governor or president—for sabotage of the incoming executive.

trespass. The archaic tort used by the ruling class to hoard wealth and prevent the masses from accessing the bounty of Gaia.

Tribe, Lawrence. A Harvard law professor who all right-thinking legal intellectuals—perhaps Tribe himself—agree should be on the United States Supreme Court.

trust. 1. To expect a third party or parties to act in your best interests rather than their own. 2. An arrangement at law that places one party (a trustee) in control of the management and disposition of property for the benefit of another (the beneficiary). This is done because the party who creates the trust does *not* trust the beneficiary. So, lack of trust begets a trust.

truth-in-sentencing. A harsh concept that requires convicted felons to remain in prison for the duration of their sentences. This replaces the system that provided time off for good behavior. The rationale for reducing the amount of time served based on good behavior of the prisoner can be expressed thus:"Behave yourself or we might make you serve all ten years of your sentence." By contrast, truth in sentencing might be expressed like this: "Behave yourself or we'll pepper spray your ugly face, toss your sorry ass in solitary confinement, and add ten years to your sentence."

trying a case on reasonable doubt. This is the phrase defense lawyers use to describe any effort to concoct an alternative explanation for every fact presented by the prosecution. The problem with this approach is that each fact by itself might be suscep-tible to an alternative explanation, but how likely is it that all the damning details are truly coincidental. On the farm, we called this bullshit.

UPTON, RITZ, & SHINE, P.C.
TRUSTS, ESTATES,
AND ASSET MANAGEMENT

ultimate. The influence of advertising-speak has applied this word to anything that might be slightly better than mediocre. As in the case of unique, because the word has become diluted, people want to beef it up, saying "that's beyond the ultimate . . ." By definition, nothing can be beyond the ultimate. Save this ultimate word for the ultimate circumstances, when, like, something is, like, totally tubular, ya know.

unambiguous. "Susceptible of but one meaning." Isn't it laughable that any dictionary sold to lawyers could contain this word?[4]

unborn widow. Another great hit of the rule against perpetuities. In this scenario, the gift is "to Sonny for life, and if he should pre-decease his wife, then to his widow for life, and upon her death to the issue of Sonny's body." Considering the male predilection for pretty young wives, the long life span of women and the ages at which men (at least in the entertainment industry) are siring children, it is reasonable to expect the gift to violate the rule. Sonny's widow might not even be born at the time of the testator's death. If the randy old goat marries a pert young woman, she could easily outlive him by more than 21 years, making the gift void.

4 Blacks Law Dictionary, 4ᵗʰ Edition

unconstitutional. That which is contrary to either a constitution or the ideological preferences of a majority of the justices applying it to a given situation.

Uniform Commercial Code. A thought- and labor-saving convention that frees lawyers from the inconvenience of drafting complete and enforceable contracts.

unique. Unique means *one of a kind*—not rare, not uncommon, not unusual, not unexpected, not occasional, not infrequent, not unwonted, not two-of-a-kind. Because it means one of a kind, by definition, it cannot be qualified. Nothing can be more, very, wildly, totally, really, truly, exceptionally, kind of, or the most unique.

United States Supreme Court. The court of final appellate jurisdiction in the American federal system. *Refer to U.S. Const. art III.* The United States Supreme Court is distinguished among its counterparts in other nations as the only court with the power to transform the personal prejudices of its members into the organic and immutable law of the land. *See judicial review.*

unjust enrichment. Any activity that allows someone to earn or save more money than you do.

usufruct. Tom's response when Tessio asked for leniency following his betrayal of the Corleone family.

usury. The prevailing credit-card interest rate minus ten percent.

VIG, COSTAS, MOORE & MOORE
BANKING, FINANCE & SECURITIES LAW

vagrant. A person over 18 years of age who, though able-bodied, does not support him- or herself through regular employment but frequents public places to solicit money from others. Most vagrancy laws were held unconstitutional because the definition applied to law students and politicians.

verified pleading. A sworn document formally declaring the allegations or defenses of a litigant, drafted to shade the truth as much as possible without actually committing perjury.

very. A feeble (not very weak) word. Very strong: herculean. Very cold: frigid. Very hot: sweltering. Very slow: glacial. Very fast: rapid. Very mean: vicious. Very kind: benevolent.

vice. 1. Recreational behavior that is considered unbecoming or unacceptable in society and which is prohibited or curtailed by law. 2. A tool affixed to a bench or similar platform that has a cam or screw that will close a set of jaws around the most delicate portions of your anatomy if your spouse finds you practicing a vice without her approval.

vig. 1. Abbreviation of vigorish, meaning profit or a commission paid to a broker, and which itself is a Yiddish version of the Russian *vyigrysh,* or winnings.

2. Loan sharks use the term to denote the interest paid or to be paid on a loan. 3. In bookmaking, the house pays out less than the amount wagered if the gambler wins. The difference between the amount of the bet and the amount paid out is the vig. That is, if the vig is 9/10 and Gus Gambler places a bet of $100 on a football game and wins, he'll get back his $100 dollar wager plus $90. If Willy Wager makes the same bet and loses, the bookie takes all $100. 4. In law, the vig is a non-refundable retainer paid when bookie, Willy, and Gus are busted for illegal gambling, money laundering, and tax evasion. (Now everyone should get the joke at the start of this section.)

voir dire. French for "to speak truth." The process of prejudicing potential jurors in favor of your client by lying to them about the case before they're seated and then excluding anyone who doesn't seem gullible enough to believe your spin.

d debt • bait and switch • bankrupt • bankruptcy •bar •bar review course • basis • bench • best evidence rule • big gun •bilious •billable hour •birdie •black
ck letter law • blue book • bogart • bogie • boiler plate • bonus • book •boot •booty • bork •bribe • bust •busted • c.a.f.o. •calendar call • chain • child sup
ming the file • circumstantial evidence •citation • class action • clearly • clients • closing costs • coffee • comparative negligence • compensatory dama
ideration • constitutional law • contract • contributory negligence • contumacious •corporation • corpus delicti • counselor • creditor • cross examination • dea
ad man's acts • deceit • deep pocket • de minimis non curat lex • demurrer • deposition • derogatory clause • devil's dictionary • dictionary, law • directed v
closure • divorce • dormant commerce clause • dorr's Rebellion • double billing • double jeopardy • due process • dying declaration • e.s.o.p. employee share ow
plan • eagle • economic development program • ego • eighth amendment •ejuration • entitlement • equal protection clause • equity • escheat •estate • es
opel, equitable • ethics • evidence, laws of / rules of • excited utterance • exclusionary rule • exculpatory evidence rule • exhaustion of remedies • ex-wif
and • face time • fair • fair use doctrine • fairway • false arrest • federal judge • federalism • federalism • federal witness protection program • federalist so
h amendment • fifteenth amendment • filibuster • first amendment • floating crap game • fourteenth amendment • fourth amendment • force majeure • fra
ege •fraud • frivolous • fruit of the poisonous tree • fundamental right • garden • general denial • gerrymander • gift causa mortis • gift tax • gloss • good sa
statutes • got my papers! • great compromise • graft • gross • guarantee clause • guilt • h.a.p. • habeas corpus • habitability • habitability, warrantee of • he
, Learned • harmless error • harvard law • hassle • hazardous • hazardous waste • headnote • hearsay • heirloom • hereinabove, hereinafter, heretofore • ho
said • homicide • hornbook • hose • hundred weight • hung jury • ill fame • immoral • impediment to marriage • import-export clause • imputed negligence • imp
orporation by reference • income • inchoate • indemnity • indigent • inevitable discovery rule • infancy • internal Revenue code • internal Revenue service •
al property • interstate commerce • ipso facto • irrelevant • jack • jeopardy • judicial review • jump • jail • jailhouse lawyer • joint and several liability • journe
ege • judgment • judgment not withstanding the verdict • jurisprudence • jury • jury instructions • jury wheel • just compensation • justice • justification • k
iver-cellars act • kentucky rule • kick • kickback • kilo • kiting • kleptomania • knock and announce • know • know-it-all • known-heirs • laches, estoppel by •
act • lapse in judgement • law • law of the case • law review • lawyer's trust account • lead counsel • legislative intent • liability • libel • link • liquidated dam
 jation • loaded • long-arm jurisdiction • lose • maintenance • malice aforethought • malicious prosecution • malpractice insurance • manual labor • making a ne
rriage • marrone • mason • matlock, ben • maundering • mcnaughton Rule • mendacity • mens rea • merely • minnesota twins, the • monopoly • mortgage
• multi-state • navigable waters • negligence • new york • new york lawyers • ninth amendment • no-knock warrant • not-for-profit corporation • nutshell • o
m • objection • obscenity • offer • old bailey • oligarchy • originalist • paternity • paternity test • palimony • penultimate • perspicuity • pike test • plea bar
ssey v. ferguson • potter, stewart • poverty law • pornography • prevarication • product liability • professional responsibility • prior inconsistent statement •
aint • prolix • public interest law • public interest lawyer • punitive damages • quantum meruit • quash • quarter section • question presented • quid pro quo •
n deed • rainmaker • rational basis test • rejection • remand • residuum • residuum rule • res ipsa loquitor • res judicata • respondent superior • responsible ch
e rule against perpetuities • screw • screw-the-pooch • second amendment • sentence • separation of powers • settlement • seventh amendment • sinking fu
enth amendment • sixth amendment • slander • solicitation • spendthrift • stare decisis • stages of marriage • statute • statutes of frauds • street lawyer •
truction • strict scrutiny • sub rosa • substantive due process • sudden heat of passion • summer associate • taylor law • take it upstairs • taxation • tenth am
• think-they-know-it-all • third amendment • tickle • title insurance • tort • to wit • traduce • trespass • trust • ultimate • unambiguous • unconstitutional • un
mercial code • unique • united states supreme court • unjust enrichment • usury • usufruct • vagrant • verified pleading • very • waiver • warhorse • war
ess • warranty, implied • warranty period • ways-and-means • webster, daniel • west publishing • whole-life insurance • wirt, william • withholding • yield •
rel • zealous representation • zone of interest test • zoning • absence of malice • accessory • accomplice • acquit • act of god • action • activist judge • actus
ministrative law • admiralty law • agent • albatross • alimony • alternative pleading • amnesty • ambulance chaser • antitrust laws • appeal • arbitrary and c
s • armed and dangerous • as is • assumpsit • attorney • b.m.w. • bad debt • bait and switch • bankrupt • bankruptcy •bar •bar review course • basis • bee
evidence rule • big gun •bilious •billable hour •birdie •black acre • black letter law • blue book • bogart • bogie • boiler plate • bonus • book •boot •booty •
e • bust •busted • c.a.f.o. •calendar call • chain • child support •churning the file • circumstantial evidence •citation • class action • clearly • clients • cl
s • coffee • comparative negligence • compensatory damages • consideration • constitutional law • contract • contributory negligence • contumacious •cor
• corpus delicti • counselor • creditor • cross examination • dead file • dead man's acts • deceit • deep pocket • de minimis non curat lex • demurrer • depo
ogatory clause • devil's dictionary • dictionary, law • directed verdict • disclosure • divorce • dormant commerce clause • dorr's Rebellion • double billing • d
ardy • due process • dying declaration • e.s.o.p. employee share ownership plan • eagle absence of malice • accessory • accomplice • acquit • act of god • a
ivist judge • actus reus • administrative law • admiralty law • agent • albatross • alimony • alternative pleading • amnesty • ambulance chaser • antitrust la
al • arbitrary and capricious • armed and dangerous • as is • assumpsit • attorney • b.m.w. • bad debt • bait and switch • bankrupt • bankruptcy •bar •bar re
se • basis • bench • best evidence rule • big gun •bilious •billable hour •birdie •black acre • black letter law • blue book • bogart • bogie • boiler plate • bon
•boot •booty • bork •bribe • bust •busted • c.a.f.o. •calendar call • chain • child support •churning the file • circumstantial evidence •citation • class act
ly • clients • closing costs • coffee • comparative negligence • compensatory damages • consideration • constitutional law • contract • contributory negliges
imacious •corporation • corpus delicti • counselor • creditor • cross examination • dead file • dead man's acts • deceit • deep pocket • de minimis non curat
irrer • deposition • derogatory clause • devil's dictionary • dictionary, law • directed verdict • disclosure • divorce • dormant commerce clause • dorr's Rebell
le billing • double jeopardy • due process • dying declaration • e.s.o.p. employee share ownership plan • eagle • economic development program • ego • e
idment •ejuration • entitlement • equal protection clause • equity • escheat •estate • estop • estoppel, equitable • ethics • evidence, laws of / rules of • ex
ance • exclusionary rule • exculpatory evidence rule • exhaustion of remedies • ex-wife/ex-husband • face time • fair • fair use doctrine • fairway • false arr
al judge • federalism • federal witness protection program • federalist society • fifth amendment • filibuster • first amendment • floating crap game • fourte
idment • fourth amendment • force majeure • franking privilege •fraud • frivolous • fruit of the poisonous tree • fundamental right • garden • general denial • g
der • • gift causa mortis • gift tax • gloss • good samaritan statues • got my papers! • great compromise • graft • gross • guarantee clause • guilt • h.a.p. • he
us • habitability • habitability, warrantee of • hack • hand, Learned • harmless error • harvard law • hassle • hazardous • hazardous waste • headnote • hear

WISE, GUY & WHACKER
ATTORNEYS
REPRESENTING A SELECT CLIENTELE
NEW CLIENTS BY REFERRAL ONLY

waiver. The reason John Kerry lost his presidential campaign.

warhorse. Warhorses are big guns who have accumulated so much money, power, and prestige that they can rest on their laurels. They rarely rouse themselves to do much legal work themselves. Instead, they assign other attorneys, including the big guns from their firms, to do their bidding. Some people underestimate warhorses by assuming they have passed their prime. This is a serious error. Rousing a warhorse to battle is like waking a sleeping dragon. By the time he returns to his slumber, nothing is left but scorched earth and the charred bones of his prey.

warranty, express. An incomprehensible barrage of legal gibberish intended to prevent the purchaser of a product from ascertaining what the seller or manufacturer is compelled to do when the item fails to function.

warranty, implied. *Caveat emptor* no more.

warranty period. A length of time slightly shorter than the expected useful life of a product.

Warren, Earl. First majority leader of the third legislative body of the United States government.

war without end. Yet another law school attempt to cut down the rule against perpetuities. A gift of real property to be given "when the war ends" violates the rule against perpetuities because the war might not end within 21 years plus the life span of a living being. Those who use this as an example of the folly of the rule must have skipped the history class that mentioned the Hundred Years War. In case you missed it, France and England squared off from 1337 to 1453, with a couple T.V. timeouts.

Wachtler, Sol. Former Chief Justice of the New York State Court of Appeals and current professor of law. He was once thought to be in the running for either the governorship of New York or nomination to the United States Supreme Court. These plans were delayed by the term he served in an alternate form of service to the state after sending intemperate letters to his former close personal associate and her daughter. However, he is now a free man and professor of law at a top-tier school, making him a symbol of the hierarchical nature of the legal profession. Law review editors everywhere rejoice! There is always room at the top for graduates of elite schools, no matter how badly they screw up.

ways and means. A standing committee of the House of Representatives, apparently comprised of people who have never written a family budget or balanced a checkbook.

Webster, Daniel. Successor to John Adams' title of obnoxious-egocentric-blowhard-lawyer-from-New England.

West Publishing. The Standard Oil of legal publishing. Through the headnotes placed in their case reporters and digests, the editors of West Publishing have more influence over law than Harvard Law School, Congress, and the Supreme Court combined.

whole life insurance. A form of life insurance policy sold as an investment. The continued ability of salespeople to convince people to buy whole life policies proves P.T. Barnum was right.[5]

Wickard v. Filburn, **317 U.S. 111 (1942).** This apology to F. D. Roosevelt following the court packing scare held that the only activity outside of Congress's power is one that will not have any affect on interstate commerce even if everyone in the nation decided to do it. Not surprisingly, since announcing this standard, the Supreme Court has

---

[5] "There's a sucker born every minute."

not discovered an activity that falls outside of the purview of Congress's power over commerce.

Wirt, William. Wirt had an amazing career. At the request of Thomas Jefferson, he prosecuted the government's case against Aaron Burr. He was appointed Attorney General by James Monroe and held the position through the administration of John Q. Adams. For someone to bridge the gap between Jefferson and the Adams clan was amazing enough, but Wirt displayed even more amazing feats of political skill. In 1832, he became the Anti-Masonic party's candidate for president despite being a prominent Free Mason, and he actually carried a state.

wise guy. One who is a participant in organized crime. The term *mafioso* fell out of favor as progressive criminal enterprises embraced the virtues of ethnic diversity.

withholding. The confiscation of money from employee pay. This turns all employers into uncompensated tax collectors for the federal government (possibly in violation of the Thirteenth Amendment). This was done because politicians realized that the revolution would be at hand if people were forced to write a check to the government for at least one-third of their annual pay.

debt • bait and switch • bankrupt • bankruptcy • bar • bar review course • basis • bench • best evidence rule • big gun •bilious •billable hour •birdie •black a
k letter law • blue book • bogart • bogie • boiler plate • bonus • book •boot •booty • bork •bribe • bust •busted • c.a.f.o. •calendar call • chain • child sup
hing the file • circumstantial evidence •citation • class action • clearly • clients • closing costs • coffee • comparative negligence • compensatory damage
eration • constitutional law • contract • contributory negligence • contumacious •corporation • corpus delicti • counselor • creditor • cross examination • dead
d man's acts • deceit • deep pocket • de minimis non curat lex • demurrer • deposition • derogatory clause • devil's dictionary • dictionary, law • directed ver
osure • divorce • dormant commerce clause • dorr's Rebellion • double billing • double jeopardy • due process • dying declaration • e.s.o.p. employee share ow
lan • eagle • economic development program • ego • eighth amendment •ejuration • entitlement • equal protection clause • equity • escheat •estate • esto
el, equitable • ethics • evidence, laws of / rules of • excited utterance • exclusionary rule • exculpatory evidence rule • exhaustion of remedies • ex-wife
nd • face time • fair • fair use doctrine • fairway • false arrest • federal judge • federalism • federalism • federal witness protection program • federalist soc
amendment • fifteenth amendment • filibuster • first amendment • floating crap game • fourteenth amendment • fourth amendment • force majeure • frank
ge •fraud • frivolous • fruit of the poisonous tree • fundamental right • garden • general denial • gerrymander • gift causa mortis • gift tax • gloss • good sar
atues • got my papers! • great compromise • graft • gross • guarantee clause • guilt • h.a.p. • habeas corpus • habitability • habitability, warrantee of • ha
Learned • harmless error • harvard law • hassle • hazardous • hazardous waste • headnote • hearsay • heirloom • hereinabove, hereinafter, heretofore • he s
id • homicide • hornbook • hose • hundred weight • hung jury • ill fame • immoral • impediment to marriage • import-export clause • imputed negligence • impe
rporation by reference • income • inchoate • indemnity • indigent • inevitable discovery rule • infancy • internal Revenue code • internal Revenue service • ir
l property • interstate commerce • ipso facto • irrelevant • jack • jeopardy • judicial review • jump • jail • jailhouse lawyer • joint and several liability • journal
ge • judgment • judgment not withstanding the verdict • jurisprudence • jury • jury instructions • jury wheel • just compensation • justice • justification • k.
er-cellars act • kentucky fried • kick • kickback • kilo • kiting • kleptomania • knock and announce • know • know-it-all • known-heirs • laches, estoppel by •
• lapse in judgement • law • law of the case • law review • lawyer's trust account • lead counsel • legislative intent • liability • link • liquidated dama
ation • loaded • long-arm jurisdiction • lose • maintenance • malice aforethought • malicious prosecution • malpractice insurance • manual labor • making a rec
iage • marrone • mason • matlock, ben • maundering • mcnaughton Rule • mendacity • mens rea • merely • minnesota twins, the • monopoly • mortgage in
• multi-state • navigable waters • negligence • new york • new york lawyers • ninth amendment • no-knock warrant • not-for-profit corporation • nutshell • ob
n • objection • obscenity • offer • old bailey • oligarchy • originalist • paternity • paternity test • palimony • penultimate • perspicuity • pike test • plea barg
sey v. ferguson • potter, stewart • poverty law • pornography • prevarication • product liability • professional responsibility • prior inconsistent statement • p
nt • prolix • public interest law • public interest lawyer • punitive damages • quantum meruit • quash • quarter section • question presented • quid pro quo • c
eed • rainmaker • rational basis test • rejection • remand • residuum • residuum rule • res ipsa loquitor • res judicata • respondent superior • responsible off
rule against perpetuities • screw • screw-the-pooch • second amendment • sentence • separation of powers • settlement • seventh amendment • sinking fun
nth amendment • sixth amendment • slander • solicitation • spendthrift • stare decisis • stages of marriage • statute • statutes of frauds • street lawyer • s
uction • strict scrutiny • sub rosa • substantive due process • sudden heat of passion • summer associate • taylor law • take it upstairs • taxation • tenth ame
• think-they-know-it-all • third amendment • tickle • title insurance • tort • to wit • traduce • trespass • trust • ultimate • unambiguous • unconstitutional • unif
ercial code • unique • united states supreme court • unjust enrichment • usury • usufruct • vagrant • verified pleading • very • waiver • warhorse • warra
s • warranty, implied • warranty period • ways-and-means • webster, daniel • west publishing • whole-life insurance • wirt, william • withholding • yield • y
l • zealous representation • zone of interest test • zoning • absence of malice • accessory • accomplice • acquit • act of god • action • activist judge • actus
inistrative law • admiralty law • agent • albatross • alimony • alternative pleading • amnesty • ambulance chaser • antitrust laws • appeal • arbitrary and ca
• armed and dangerous • as is • assumpsit • attorney • b.m.w. • bad debt • bait and switch • bankrupt • bankruptcy •bar •bar review course • basis • benc
vidence rule • big gun •bilious •billable hour •birdie •black acre • black letter law • blue book • bogart • bogie • boiler plate • bonus • book •boot •booty • b
• bust •busted • c.a.f.o. •calendar call • chain • child support •churning the file • circumstantial evidence •citation • class action • clearly • clients • clos
• coffee • comparative negligence • compensatorY damages • consideration • constitutional law • contract • contributory negligence • contumacious •corp
corpus delicti • counselor • creditor • cross examination • dead file • dead man's acts • deceit • deep pocket • de minimis non curat lex • demurrer • deposi
gatory clause • devil's dictionary • dictionary, law • directed verdict • disclosure • divorce • dormant commerce clause • dorr's Rebellion • double billing • dou
dy • due process • dying declaration • e.s.o.p. employee share ownership plan • eagle absence of malice • accessory • accomplice • acquit • act of god • a
rist judge • actus reus • administrative law • admiralty law • agent • albatross • alimony • alternative pleading • amnesty • ambulance chaser • antitrust law
l • arbitrary and capricious • armed and dangerous • as is • assumpsit • attorney • b.m.w. • bad debt • bait and switch • bankrupt • bankruptcy •bar •bar rev
• basis • bench • best evidence rule • big gun •bilious •billable hour •birdie •black acre • black letter law • blue book • bogart • bogie • boiler plate • bon
boot •booty • bork •bribe • bust •busted • c.a.f.o •calendar call • chain • child support •churning the file • circumstantial evidence •citation • class actio
• clients • closing costs • coffee • comparative negligence • compensatory damages • consideration • constitutional law • contract • contributory negligenc
macious •corporation • corpus delicti • counselor • creditor • cross examination • dead file • dead man's acts • deceit • deep pocket • de minimis non curat le
rer • deposition • derogatory clause • devil's dictionary • dictionary, law • directed verdict • disclosure • divorce • dormant commerce clause • dorr's Rebelli
e billing • double jeopardy • due process • dying declaration • e.s.o.p. employee share ownership plan • eagle • economic development program • ego • eig
dment •ejuration • entitlement • equal protection clause • equity • escheat •estate • estop • estoppel, equitable • ethics • evidence, laws of / rules of • exc
nce • exclusionary rule • exculpatory evidence rule • exhaustion of remedies • ex-wife/ex-husband • face time • fair • fair use doctrine • fairway • false arre
l judge • federalism • federal witness protection program • federalist society • fifth amendment • filibuster • first amendment • floating crap game • fourtee
dment • fourth amendment • force majeure • franking privilege •fraud • frivolous • fruit of the poisonous tree • fundamental right • garden • general denial •
or • gift causa mortis • gift tax • gloss • good samaritan statues • got my papers! • great compromise • graft • gross • guarantee clause • guilt • h.a.p. • hab
s • habitability, warrantee of • hack • hand, Learned • harmless error • harvard law • hassle • hazardous • hazardous waste • headnote • hearsa

YAK, BOOT, AND HURELY
D.W.I. DEFENSE

yield. 1. To let another pass or act. 2. An amount resulting from an effort or process. For example, failure to obey a traffic sign at an intersection results in two demerit points marked on your driver's license; that is, failure to yield yields.

yikes. The sound of a client being told the amount their prospective attorney expects as a retainer.

yokel. A client with a dubious claim and not enough money to pay in full.

ZONNE & AUT
LSAT PREPARATION
THROUGH LECTURES,
PRACTICE TESTS,
AND
RIGOROUS MEMORIZATION

zealous representation. A phrase used by pathologically competitive lawyers to justify their utterly reprehensible behavior.

zone of interest test. A judicially created limitation of federal jurisdiction that requires plaintiffs to establish that they are within "the zone of interest" intended to be protected by the law pursuant to which they have brought suit. This reduces the number of cases on the docket and allows judges to weed out plaintiffs who are using a statute just to be obnoxious pains in the ass.

zoning. 1. Local laws used by people who have purchased desirable real estate to exclude all others from obtaining it too. 2. The act of entering a meditative state induced by interminable lectures, meetings, speeches, or presentations. To wit: droning causes zoning.

debt • bait and switch • bankrupt • bankruptcy •bar •bar review course • basis • bench • best evidence rule • big gun •bilious •billable hour •birdie •blac
ack letter law • blue book • bogart • bogie • boiler plate • bonus • book •boot •booty • bork •bribe • bust •busted • c.a.f.o. •calendar call • chain • child s
rning the file • circumstantial evidence •citation • class action • clearly • clients • closing costs • coffee • comparative negligence • compensatory dama
sideration • constitutional law • contract • contributory negligence • contumacious •corporation • corpus delicti • counselor • creditor • cross examination • de
ad man's acts • deceit • deep pocket • de minimis non curat lex • demurrer • deposition • derogatory clause • devil's dictionary • dictionary, law • directed v
sclosure • divorce • dormant commerce clause • dorr's Rebellion • double billing • double jeopardy • due process • dying declaration • e.s.o.p. employee share o
plan • eagle • economic development program • ego • eighth amendment •ejuration • entitlement • equal protection clause • equity • escheat •estate • e
ppel, equitable • ethics • evidence, laws of / rules of • excited utterance • exclusionary rule • exculpatory evidence rule • exhaustion of remedies • ex-wi
and • face time • fair • fair use doctrine • fairway • false arrest • federal judge • federalism • federalism • federal witness protection program • federalist s
th amendment • fifteenth amendment • filibuster • first amendment • floating crap game • fourteenth amendment • fourth amendment • force majeure • fra
lege •fraud • frivolous • fruit of the poisonous tree • fundamental right • garden • general denial • gerrymander • gift causa mortis • gift tax • gloss • good s
statues • got my papers! • great compromise • graft • gross • guarantee clause • guilt • h.a.p. • habeas corpus • habitability • habitability, warrantee of • I
I, Learned • harmless error • harvard law • hassle • hazardous • hazardous waste • headnote • hearsay • heirloom • hereinabove, hereinafter, heretofore • he
said • homicide • hornbook • hose • hundred weight • hung jury • ill fame • immoral • impediment to marriage • import-export clause • imputed negligence • in
corporation by reference • income • inchoate • indemnity • indigent • inevitable discovery rule • infancy • internal Revenue code • internal Revenue service •
ual property • interstate commerce • ipso facto • irrelevant • jack • jeopardy • judicial review • jump • jail • jailhouse lawyer • joint and several liability • journ
lege • judgment • judgment not withstanding the verdict • jurisprudence • jury • jury instructions • jury wheel • just compensation • justice • justification •
uver-cellars act • kentucky rule • kick • kickback • kilo • kiting • kleptomania • knock and announce • know • know-it-all • known-heirs • laches, estoppel by
ract • lapse in judgement • law • law of the case • law review • lawyer's trust account • lead counsel • legislative intent • liability • libel • link • liquidated dam
igation • loaded • long-arm jurisdiction • lose • maintenance • malice aforethought • malicious prosecution • malpractice insurance • manual labor • making a
arriage • marrone • mason • matlock, ben • maundering • mcnaughton Rule • mendacity • mens rea • merely • minnesota twins, the • monopoly • mortgage
a • multi-state • navigable waters • negligence • new york • new york lawyers • ninth amendment • no-knock warrant • not-for-profit corporation • nutshell
um • objection • obscenity • offer • old bailey • oligarchy • originalist • paternity • paternity test • palimony • penultimate • perspicuity • pike test • plea b
essey v. ferguson • potter, stewart • poverty law • pornography • prevarication • product liability • professional responsibility • prior inconsistent statement •
raint • prolix • public interest law • public interest lawyer • punitive damages • quantum meruit • quash • quartet section • question presented • quid pro quo •
n deed • rainmaker • rational basis test • rejection • remand • residuum • residuum rule • res ipsa loquitor • res judicata • respondent superior • responsible •
• rule against perpetuities • screw • screw-the-pooch • second amendment • sentence • separation of powers • settlement • seventh amendment • sinking
nenth amendment • sixth amendment • slander • solicitation • spendthrift • stare decisis • stages of marriage • statute • statutes of frauds • street lawyer •
struction • strict scrutiny • sub rosa • substantive due process • sudden heat of passion • summer associate • taylor law • take it upstairs • taxation • tenth a
t • think-they-know-it-all • third amendment • tickle • title insurance • tort • to wit • traduce • trespass • trust • ultimate • unambiguous • unconstitutional • ul
mercial code • unique • united states supreme court • unjust enrichment • usury • usufruct • vagrant • verified pleading • very • waiver • warhorse • wa
ess • warranty, implied • warranty period • ways-and-means • webster, daniel • west publishing • whole-life insurance • wirt, william • withholding • yield •
kel • zealous representation • zone of interest test • zoning • absence of malice • accessory • accomplice • acquit • act of god • action • activist judge • actu
ministrative law • admiralty law • agent • albatross • alimony • alternative pleading • amnesty • ambulance chaser • antitrust laws • appeal • arbitrary and
s • armed and dangerous • as is • assumpsit • attorney • b.m.w. • bad debt • bait and switch • bankrupt • bankruptcy •bar •bar review course • basis • be
evidence rule • big gun •bilious •billable hour •birdie •black acre • black letter law • blue book • bogart • bogie • boiler plate • bonus • book •boot •booty
be • bust •busted • c.a.f.o. •calendar call • chain • child support •churning the file • circumstantial evidence •citation • class action • clearly • clients • cl
s • coffee • comparative negligence • compensatoFy damages • consideration • constitutional law • contract • contributory negligence • contumacious •cor
• corpus delicti • counselor • creditor • cross examination • dead file • dead man's acts • deceit • deep pocket • de minimis non curat lex • demurrer • depo
rogatory clause • devil's dictionary • dictionary, law • directed verdict • disclosure • divorce • dormant commerce clause • dorr's Rebellion • double billing • d
ardy • due process • dying declaration • e.s.o.p. employee share ownership plan • eagle absence of malice • accessory • accomplice • acquit • act of god •
tivist judge • actus reus • administrative law • admiralty law • agent • albatross • alimony • alternative pleading • amnesty • ambulance chaser • antitrust l
al • arbitrary and capricious • armed and dangerous • as is • assumpsit • attorney • b.m.w. • bad debt • bait and switch • bankrupt • bankruptcy •bar •bar r
se • basis • bench • best evidence rule • big gun •bilious •billable hour •birdie •black acre • black letter law • blue book • bogart • bogie • boiler plate • bo
c •boot •booty • bork •bribe • bust •busted • c.a.f.o. •calendar call • chain • child support •churning the file • circumstantial evidence •citation • class ac
rly • clients • closing costs • coffee • comparative negligence • compensatory damages • consideration • constitutional law • contract • contributory
umacious •corporation • corpus delicti • counselor • creditor • cross examination • dead file • dead man's acts • deceit • deep pocket • de minimis non cura
urrer • deposition • derogatory clause • devil's dictionary • dictionary, law • directed verdict • disclosure • divorce • dormant commerce clause • dorr's Rebel
ble billing • double jeopardy • due process • dying declaration • e.s.o.p. employee share ownership plan • eagle • economic development program • ego •
ndment •ejuration • entitlement • equal protection clause • equity • escheat •estate • estop • estoppel, equitable • ethics • evidence, laws of / rules of • e
ance • exclusionary rule • exculpatory evidence rule • exhaustion of remedies • ex-wife/ex-husband • face time • fair • fair use doctrine • fairway • false ar
ral judge • federalism • federal witness protection program • federalist society • fifth amendment • filibuster • first amendment • floating crap game • four
ndment • fourth amendment • force majeure • franking privilege •fraud • frivolous • fruit of the poisonous tree • fundamental right • garden • general denial •
der • gift causa mortis • gift tax • gloss • good samaritan statues • got my papers! • great compromise • graft • gross • guarantee clause • guilt • h.a.p. • h
us • habitability • habitability, warrantee of • hack, hand, Learned • harmless error • harvard law • hassle • hazardous • hazardous waste • headnote • hea

...rous pleading • anxiously • antecedent debtor • antitrust laws • appeal • arbitrary and capricious • armed and dangerous • as is • assumpsit • attorney • b.m...

debt • bait and switch • bankrupt • bankruptcy • bar •bar review course • basis • bench • best evidence rule • big gun •bilious •billable hour • birdie •black a

k letter law • blue book • bogart • bogie • boiler plate • bonus • book •boot •booty • bork •bribe • bust • busted • c.a.f.o. •calendar call • chain • child sup

ning the file • circumstantial evidence •citation • class action • clearly • clients • closing costs • coffee • comparative negligence • compensatory damage

eration • constitutional law • contract • contributory negligence • contumacious •corporation • corpus delicti • counselor • creditor • cross examination • dead

l man's acts • deceit • deep pocket • de minimis non curat lex • demurrer • deposition • derogatory clause • devil's dictionary • dictionary, law • directed ver

osure • divorce • dormant commerce clause • dorr's Rebellion • double billing • double jeopardy • due process • dying declaration • e.s.o.p. employee share ow

lan • eagle • economic development program • ego • eighth amendment • ejuration • entitlement • equal protection clause • equity • escheat • estate • esto

el, equitable • ethics • evidence, laws of / rules of • excited utterance • exclusionary rule • exculpatory evidence rule • exhaustion of remedies • ex-wife

nd • face time • fair • fair use doctrine • fairway • false arrest • federal judge • federalism • federalism • federal witness protection program • federalist soc

amendment • fifteenth amendment • filibuster • first amendment • floating crap game • fourteenth amendment • fourth amendment • force majeure • fran

ge •fraud • frivolous • fruit of the poisonous tree • fundamental right • garden • general denial • gerrymander • gift causa mortis • gift tax • gloss • good sar

atues • got my papers! • great compromise • graft • gross • guarantee clause • guilt • h.a.p. • habeas corpus • habitability • habitability, warrantee of • hac

Learned • harmless error • harvard law • hassle • hazardous • hazardous waste • headnote • hearsay • heirloom • hereinabove, hereinafter, heretofore • he s

id • homicide • hornbook • hose • hundred weight • hung jury • ill fame • immoral • impediment to marriage • import-export clause • imputed negligence • impe

rporation by reference • income • inchoate • indemnity • indigent • inevitable discovery rule • infancy • internal Revenue code • internal Revenue service • ir

l property • interstate commerce • ipso facto • irrelevant • jack • jeopardy • judicial review • jump • jail • jailhouse lawyer • joint and several liability • journa

ge • judgment • judgment not withstanding the verdict • jurisprudence • jury • jury instructions • jury wheel • just compensation • justice • justification • k

ver-cellars act • kentucky rule • kick • kickback • kilo • kiting • kleptomania • knock and announce • know • know-it-all • known-heirs • laches, estoppel by • l

ct • lapse in judgement • law • law of the case • law review • lawyer's trust account • lead counsel • legislative intent • liability • libel • link • liquidated dama

ation • loaded • long-arm jurisdiction • lose • maintenance • malice • malice aforethought • malicious prosecution • malpractice insurance • manual labor • making a re

iage • marrone • mason • matlock, ben • maundering • mcnaughton Rule • mendacity • mens rea • merely • minnesota twins, the • monopoly • mortgage in

• multi-state • navigable waters • negligence • new york • new york lawyers • ninth amendment • no-knock warrant • not-for-profit corporation • nutshell • ot

1 • objection • obscenity • offer • old bailey • oligarchy • originalist • paternity • paternity test • palimony • penultimate • perspicuity • pike test • plea bar

sey v. ferguson • potter, stewart • poverty law • pornography • prevarication • product liability • professional responsibility • prior inconsistent statement • p

nt • prolix • public interest law • public interest lawyer • punitive damages • quantum meruit • quash • quarter section • question presented • quid pro quo • c

deed • rainmaker • rational basis test • rejection • remand • residuum • residuum rule • res ipsa loquitor • res judicata • respondent superior • responsible off

rule against perpetuities • screw • screw-the-pooch • second amendment • sentence • separation of powers • settlement • seventh amendment • sinking fu

nth amendment • sixth amendment • slander • solicitation • spendthrift • stare decisis • stages of marriage • statute • statutes of frauds • street lawyer • s

uction • strict scrutiny • sub rosa • substantive due process • sudden heat of passion • summer associate • taylor law • take it upstairs • taxation • tenth ame

• think-they-know-it-all • third amendment • tickle • title insurance • tort • to wit • traduce • trespass • trust • ultimate • unambiguous • unconstitutional • unif

ercial code • unique • united states supreme court • unjust enrichment • usury • usufruct • vagrant • verified pleading • very • waiver • warhorse • warra

s • warranty, implied • warranty period • ways-and-means • webster, daniel • west publishing • whole-life insurance • wirt, william • withholding • yield • y

el • zealous representation • zone of interest test • zoning • absence of malice • accessory • accomplice • acquit • act of god • action • activist judge • actus

inistrative law • admiralty law • agent • albatross • alimony • alternative pleading • amnesty • ambulance chaser • antitrust laws • appeal • arbitrary and ca

• armed and dangerous • as is • assumpsit • attorney • b.m.w. • bad debt • bait and switch • bankrupt • bankruptcy •bar •bar review course • basis • bene

vidence rule • big gun •bilious •billable hour •birdie •black acre • black letter law • blue book • bogart • bogie • boiler plate • bonus • book •boot •booty •

• bust •busted • c.a.f.o. •calendar call • chain • child support •churning the file • circumstantial evidence •citation • class action • clearly • clients • clo

• coffee • comparative negligence • compensatorFy damages • consideration • constitutional law • contract • contributory negligence • contumacious •corp

corpus delicti • counselor • creditor • cross examination • dead file • dead man's acts • deceit • deep pocket • de minimis non curat lex • demurrer • deposi

gatory clause • devil's dictionary • dictionary, law • directed verdict • disclosure • divorce • dormant commerce clause • dorr's Rebellion • double billing • do

dy • due process • dying declaration • e.s.o.p. employee share ownership plan • eagle absence of malice • accessory • accomplice • acquit • act of god • ac

vist judge • actus reus • administrative law • admiralty law • agent • albatross • alimony • alternative pleading • amnesty • ambulance chaser • antitrust law

l • arbitrary and capricious • armed and dangerous • as is • assumpsit • attorney • b.m.w • bad debt • bait and switch • bankrupt • bankruptcy •bar •bar rev

e • basis • bench • best evidence rule • big gun •bilious •billable hour •birdie •black acre • black letter law • blue book • bogart • bogie • boiler plate • bon

•boot •booty • bork •bribe • bust •busted • c.a.f.o. •calendar call • chain • child support •churning the file • circumstantial evidence •citation • class actio

r • clients • closing costs • coffee • comparative negligence • compensatory damages • consideration • constitutional law • contract • contributory negligen

macious •corporation • corpus delicti • counselor • creditor • cross examination • dead file • dead man's acts • deceit • deep pocket • de minimis non curat l

rer • deposition • derogatory clause • devil's dictionary • dictionary, law • directed verdict • disclosure • divorce • dormant commerce clause • dorr's Rebelli

billing • double jeopardy • due process • dying declaration • e.s.o.p. employee share ownership plan • eagle • economic development program • ego • eig

dment • ejuration • entitlement • equal protection clause • equity • escheat • estate • estop • estoppel, equitable • ethics • evidence, laws of / rules of • exc

nce • exclusionary rule • exculpatory evidence rule • exhaustion of remedies • ex-wife/ex-husband • face time • fair • fair use doctrine • fairway • false arre

l judge • federalism • federal witness protection program • federalist society • fifth amendment • filibuster • first amendment • floating crap game • fourte

dment • fourth amendment • force majeure • franking privilege •fraud • frivolous • fruit of the poisonous tree • fundamental right • garden • general denial • ge

er • gift causa mortis • gift tax • gloss • good samaritan statues • got my papers! • great compromise • graft • gross • guarantee clause • guilt • h.a.p. • habe

s • habitability • habitability, warrantee of • hack • hand, Learned • harmless error • harvard law • hassle • hazardous • hazardous waste • headnote • hears

APPENDIX A:
An Abridged Taxonomy of Lawyers

Most lawyers are considerate, reasonable, and professional. Despite the tension of the adversarial system, they maintain civil relationships. Unfortunately, the practice of law also provides a haven for individuals with personality traits that can charitably be described as unpleasant. Just as the full spectrum of color in a television picture comes from different combinations of blue, red, and cyan, varying amounts of arrogance, insecurity, and greed combine to form an infinite variety of obnoxious lawyers. The following taxonomy describes common types of annoying lawyer personalities and how to deal with them.

1. Think-They-Know-It-Alls

Attorneys who think they know it all are common, but relatively non-toxic to other attorneys. Thinking you know everything, or appearing as though you do, is an occupational hazard of practicing law. Being decisive and knowledgeable are virtues of good attorneys. Clients pay attorneys for answers and expect them to be delivered with confidence. However, knowing when you need to research, listen, and learn is also a critical component of being a good lawyer. This is where think-they-know-it-alls fail.

Thinking you know it all happens when you forcefully state positions or opinions about topics on which you are wholly or partially ignorant. Why would people hold forth on subjects about which they are ignorant? Because they are accustomed to reasoning by extrapolation or deduction and completely trust their own conclusions. They start with a tidbit of knowledge and quickly concoct a doctoral thesis.

Think of *Harry Potter and the Sorcerer's Stone.* (If you have not read it, please do so now; it won't take long.) A vindictive teacher, Professor Snape, abuses Harry on his first day at school by asking a series of questions to which Harry could not reasonably know the answer. He forces Harry to say, "I don't know, sir," again and again. This is called the Socratic method, and law students endure it every day.

Schools have us conditioned to bark out answers like Pavlov's dogs. Throughout formal education, if you get the answer right you earn a gold star, a big cheerful "A" on your paper, or the approbation of the most important people in your life. Ignorance earns a red "F," ridicule from classmates, extra work, and disappointment from parents. After twelve to twenty years of this professional conditioning, it is a miracle that anyone has the mettle to utter the words "I don't know."

The danger of acting as if you know more than you do continues after law school. Attorneys who commonly work with engineers, psychologists, doctors, and other experts develop a special case of thinking they know it all. They learn the jargon and general concepts applied by these experts. After repeatedly hearing an expert give an opinion on the same topic, attorneys may think they understand the field well enough to draw conclusions on their own. Remember, a little knowledge is a dangerous thing.

Working with experts can give lawyers genuine knowledge of a topic outside the scope of their formal education. This sets the trap for the unwary. Anecdotal knowledge of a topic may let a non-expert identify an issue in a particular field of science or art. Having seen experts talk about the same issue a dozen times, a lawyer may compare the facts to those of prior cases and draw a conclusion. This is the siren song of hubris. In most fields, the real expert examines the matter according to objective methods and standards of their field to draw a case-specific conclusion. This is far different from anecdotal comparisons.

Hubris expertus manifests itself most often under four situations: when talking to a client without an expert present; during discussions with other attorneys, especially in settlement negotiations; during cross-examination; and, when presenting an argument to a judge. During any of these situations, beware the temptation to utter a professional opinion unrelated to the law.

Some attorneys manifest symptoms of thinking they know it all as a tactic to intimidate other attorneys. It is calculated bluffing. In their mind, they are Cool Hand Luke raising the bet, chasing the kid out of the poker game even though they have a deuce low kangaroo straight. When an opposing attorney holds forth about his past experience and how poorly their opponents fared, do not lose your nerve. Stay calm. Be brave. Wait for the signs.

2. Know-it-Alls

Some people really do know it all, at least in their particular field. True know-it-alls come in two types: those who think everyone is as smart and knowledgeable as they are and those who realize that most people are dullards. Those who think everyone shares their lofty intellect tend to carry the conversation if you occasionally nod and interject "I suppose so" or "isn't that a flaw in the paradigm?" The majority of true know-it-alls know they're alone in a world of morons. This category can be subdivided into two groups:

1) Pleasant people who suffer the existence of mere mortals with saintly patience, and

2) Patronizing, insufferable jerks.

If your opposing counsel is a true know-it all, do not panic. Take deep breaths and worry about your case, not about opposing counsel. Remember that you are presenting your case to ordinary people. Making the complex comprehensible will require hard work and some genius of your own, but making the judge or the jury think, "hey, it doesn't take a genius to figure this out" neutralizes the know-it-all's main advantage. It helps if your client is a nun and the opposing party is Attila the Hun.

3. Crusaders

Crusaders feel their client's pain, even if the client does not have any. Each of their clients suffers wrongfully from every slight, insult, or injustice that has taken place since the campaign of genocide against Neanderthals by the imperialist Cro-Magnon.

Most crusaders work for legal aide, the public defender's office, or public interest organizations. Some start in government but soon quit because the agencies they work for "sacrifice justice on the alter of expediency."

To lawyers who have clients that pay for their services, a settlement is "a mutually acceptable compromise that lets them get on with their lives."[6] To the crusader, any settlement is "a sellout" that "perpetuates injustice."

When crusaders become disillusioned, they quit and go to work for Lie, Fleece and Steele, mega-firm. They continue to work for social justice "from the inside" by double-billing their wealthy clients. If their consciences prick them, they recommend that the firm assign one of the less promising summer interns to work on a pro bono case.

---

[6] Translation: "Holy Excrement! The litigation retainer is fifty thousand! Is their last offer still on the table?"

While billing her clients an even five hundred dollars an hour, the crusader cashes in by writing a hard-hitting expose about "the system." Her hometown library and her parents each buy a copy. The other fifty thousand copies are shredded and burned in a waste-to-energy facility on Long Island. When she finds out, she sues the publisher because dioxin from the incinerator contaminated the mother's milk of Greenland's indigenous people.

Here is a typical example of a settlement negotiation with a crusader. Your clients build and install modular homes. They also offer financing. They sold a fifty-five thousand dollar home to Mr. and Mrs. Deadbeat. The Deadbeats put down five thousand dollars and your client financed the balance with a purchase money mortgage. The client became your client three months after the Deadbeats stopped paying the loan. That is to say, four months after the down payment.

You write a demand letter, but the Deadbeats ignore it. You begin drafting pleadings. Before you put the caption on the complaint, your client storms into the office waving an order to show cause, notice of hearing, complaint, a ten-page discovery demand, and a temporary restraining order. The Deadbeats went to legal aid. Legal aid found that the loan agreement had miscalculated the actual amount of principal that would be paid over the life of the loan. The loan payment was properly calculated, and the initial balance and amortization table were included, but the total cost of the loan contained a typo. Being equitably minded people interested only in justice, they sued your client for violating the Fair Lending Standards Act.

The temporary restraining order enjoins your client from foreclosing or attempting to collect any of the amount due. Meanwhile, the Deadbeats have stripped the house of everything of value (electric fixtures, wiring, plumbing, windows, hardwood floors, kitchen cabinets, built-in appliances, etc.) and sold it. The police think it's a crack house, and the local building inspector wants it condemned. You call on legal aid to talk settlement.

"No settlement," you are told. "Your client engaged in predatory lending, and we want full damages."

"But your clients have lived rent-free for four months and destroyed the house," you complain. "How can they claim to be damaged?"

"The law requires disclosure of the total amount to be paid," she says as if talking to a fifth grader.

"It was a harmless printing error," you whine.

"They aren't educated people. Your client duped them into signing a loan they couldn't afford," she replies.

"The contract clearly and correctly stated the monthly payment," you say while waving the loan papers wildly through the air. "Never making a payment demonstrates they intended to defraud my client!"

"I'll have to report your ethical violations to the bar association," the crusader says, rising to leave. "Now, if you are done wasting *my* time, I have a heavy case load."

"What! What ethical violation," you wail, resisting the effort to strangle the smug son-of-a-bitch.

"Threatening criminal prosecution to force my client to settle their just claims," the crusader coos like a dove. "Too bad. I heard you were a good lawyer." And with that parting shot, she slouches out of the office.

A month later, you sit in front of a panel from the grievance committee explaining that you never said anything about criminal prosecution. They will call it a subtle distinction, then vote to issue a letter of reprimand. Just when you think you've hit bottom, you are personally named in a federal lawsuit that alleges you used state law to deprive the crusader's clients of "their constitutionally guaranteed right to due process."

The next day you buy a Hummer, shoot a spotted owl, and send $1,000 to Pat Buchanan's presidential campaign committee.

There are two ways of dealing with the crusader. Both require nerves of steel.

If you have the patience of a Zen master, you can roll with the punches. Never get angry, annoyed, or excited in the presence of a crusader. Most of them are masters of passive-aggressive behaviors. Aggravating people gives a crusader the gratification that normal people derive from the physical expression of romantic love.

The other method requires a gun, a glass of whiskey, and two bullets.

4. File Churners

Some attorneys view clients as a natural resource that the law firm processes into cash, sports cars, vacation homes, and attractive young companions. People have many different names for this type of attorney. Most involve parasites and human blood. Despite their drawbacks, this type of attorney also has many virtues. They often do great work on behalf of their clients. They will take any case, no matter how unpopular. Their zeal and exertion know no bounds. They will research and brief the most minute point of law and investigate every fact twice.

Unfortunately, they will also make pointless phone calls, repeatedly schedule unnecessary meetings, and prepare extensive briefs for simple matters that can be easily resolved. Having multiple attorneys work on one simple case is another classic maneuver. Lawyers and experienced clients call these tactics churning the file.

Unfortunately, one man's wasted effort is another man's diligent attention to detail. Like doctors who order every test under the sun "just to be sure," lawyers worry about being sued for malpractice. If they overlook something, it could easily come back to bite them. So, file churning is difficult to spot. It can be a matter of judgment. If a client failed to report several million dollars in taxable income, having the firm's tax expert and their top criminal litigator work together would be prudent. If Aunt Sophie is given a ticket for littering in the park, having two associates and a senior partner conference with the District Attorney would be bilking the client.

Obviously, the leeches who genuinely churn their files are stealing from their clients. Worse, file churners waste your time and inflate your clients' legal fees because you have to respond to a barrage of useless briefs, motions, and phone calls.

Technology has created an explosion in file churning. Aeons ago, in the carbon age, lawyers crafted documents one at a time. Each letter required dictation and typing. A lawyer invested labor in every word. Personal computers and laser printers put an end to that. Template documents and merge files mean that after an initial investment of twenty minutes, a document can be reproduced hundreds of time with minor revision. Now, email has eliminated the cost of ink and paper. Attorneys who cannot find real work to occupy their time can churn out hundreds of pages of pointless drivel. The real mark of a file churner is someone who insists on sending five emails an hour, but who walks to the law library to Shepardize cases manually even though the firm has unlimited access to Westlaw or Lexis/Nexis.

Professional courtesy and discretion prohibit attorneys from telling an opposing counsel's clients that they are being bilked. For example, you attend a meeting to discuss revisions to a contract. The other side has been peppering you with pointless phone calls and emails for a week. An identical negotiation last week required three phone calls, two emails, and one FedEx delivery. The other party walks into the meeting with three attorneys.

"My God! This guy is paying ten dollars a minute for these clowns to be here. Calling 1-900-XXX would be cheaper and more meaningful than this meeting," you think. When the lawyers introduce you to their client, you are bursting to say something. Remember, discretion is the better part of professional advancement.

First, you cannot be certain that your opponent plans to bill the client for presence of the extra lawyers or if the client is related to any of the people in the room. More importantly, you never can tell when one of them will be elected or appointed to a judgeship. (Try getting clients after losing thirty consecutive trials.)

5. Fish-Out-of-Water

Fortunately for lawyers, state and federal government exist to enact and enforce laws. This creates a demand for legal specialization. We have patent lawyers, tax lawyers, bankruptcy lawyers, environmental lawyers, employment lawyers, business lawyers, securities lawyers, municipal lawyers, and so forth. Some specialties have subspecialties, such as environmental lawyers who handle only Clean Air Act cases. This is how the country absorbs the ever-increasing number of law school graduates. At some point in time, the economy will consist of nothing but lawyers seeking the services of other lawyers regarding their particular specialization.

With few exceptions, anyone who passes the bar can pass him- or herself off as an expert in a particular field of law. Most lawyers are smart enough to avoid areas of law they do not understand. This may be professionalism, but it is more likely that people are lazy. Learning a new area of law takes a great deal of time and effort, so most people stay within their niche.

Occasionally, a general practitioner will try to help a client with a problem involving a highly specialized area of law, or an elected official will need to find a job for a relative who recently passed the bar. These fish-out-of-water have a universal capacity to infuriate specialists. The fish-out-of-water is so ignorant that voodoo would have a better chance of helping their clients. Worse, their presumption of competence insults the specialist who spent two years earning an L.L.M. in tax law and ten years working for the I.R.S. just so she can explain adjusted gross income to her opponent.

Innoculate yourself against becoming a fish-out-of-water by specializing. Attorneys who think of themselves as specialists rarely handle matters outside of their expertise, even if the matter is routine.

Specialists think of anything off-topic as a waste of their talents.

Rejecting work gives them an ego-induced high better than drinking a margarita that had been left unattended at a singles bar.

"I'm sorry," they giggle. "I specialize in toxic tort litigation. I'll refer you Depo, Tician & Settle, LLP. *They* handle whiplash cases all the time."

Even if you intend to open a small town general practice, identify those areas of law you will handle as a general practitioner, such as wills, estates, real estate closings, divorce, and so forth. Refer anything outside your area of practice to a specialist. Think of a doctor in a family practice. He should recognize the symptoms of heart disease, but refer the patient to a specialist for the triple-bypass.

Young attorneys desperate to pay their bills and build a practice will find it tough to turn away a customer. Join the local bar association, network with the other attorneys, and find out who does what. If you refer business to another attorney who handles cases that you do not want, reciprocity should develop. Eventually, you should earn a reputation for expertise in particular areas of law, and that will enhance your business.

169

Theoretically, when you encounter a fish-out-of-water, you should have an easy win. Practically speaking, to achieve a contract, settlement, or a win in litigation, you will have to provide countless hours of free continuing legal education. The fish-out-of-water will not advise his or her client to settle or enter a contract until (s)he understands the applicable law, and the fastest way to make that happen is to give a free lesson. In litigation, you can't ignore some moronic position espoused by the fish-out-of-water because the judge is probably a fish-out-of-water too. This is a colossal waste of time and your client pays for it. But, tempting as it may be to tell the other party his attorney is an incompetent twerp, this opens you to slander. Even though truth is the ultimate defense, it is better to waste your client's money than to become a defendant in a tort suit.

6. Do Nothings

Employers of all stripes, including law firms, love to give employees personality-type indicator tests. The people promoting these tests claim they will increase productivity by letting workers and managers understand how their coworkers and employees think. For example, a spineless kiss-ass who cannot make a decision becomes "an intuitive extrovert who focuses on building interpersonal relationships." The quest to find value in alternative perspectives and approaches does not change reality. In reality, clients pay lawyers to get results—not to make opposing parties feel good about themselves, not to schmooze with opposing counsel about their golf game, and not to try to win cases by whining about the tragic turns of life.

If you take one of these personality tests and it says you are intuitive and empathetic, you have two options:

    1) quit, or

    2) run for political office.

The most common complaint lodged against attorneys is neglect, which is legalese for "that damn lawyer hasn't done a thing." Various excuses exist for this. Some lawyers take more work than they can handle. Fear of losing or making a mistake paralyzes others. Some are just lazy.

If your boss cannot make it through his day without consulting Doctor Laura, Doctor Phil, and his horoscope, you may have to point the way to success. During the Peninsular campaign, the Union Army came to a creek. General McClellan stopped the advance while his staff debated if the creek was too deep to ford. As the cream of the Union's military argued about the depth of the waters, a young cavalry officer rode his horse to the middle of the stream and called out, "It's this deep, General."

When dealing with an opposing attorney who does nothing, taking the initiative will usually drive them forward. Set deadlines and stick to them. If that involves filing a complaint, a motion to compel, or a default, so be it. Make it known that you are a stickler for deadlines and people will be less likely to string you along.

7. The Redneck in the White Collar

Some people, particularly men, think that they can bond with others by adopting their quaint folkways. For example, the head of one large organization regaled anyone who would listen with stories about fishing and hunting. He laced his everyday speech with phrases such as, "that dog won't hunt." He eschewed suits and often wore Dickies or blue jeans. He also used European shotguns, bought top-of-the-line Orvis fly fishing gear, and collected sports cars.

No authentic hick totes around a five thousand dollar Italian gun. A hick may have five or ten cars, but only a couple of them run, and none of them are housed in a heated garage. Worse, the phrase "that dog won't hunt" probably originated in Hollywood, where some screenwriter thought it up to make a formulaic rural character seem "authentic."

Being folksy to connect with people almost always backfires because hicks are unrefined—not stupid. They know they are being patronized and lied to when someone assumes their mannerisms. Mom was right when she advised you to just be yourself.

Because the redneck in the white collar feigns a lack of sophistication, he can lull you into a false sense of superiority. In all likelihood, that "aw shucks" attitude hides someone who spends 18 hours a day, every day, reading the federal register and studying opinions of the federal courts. Do not let your guard down. Getting snookered by a buffoon would be truly embarrasing.

d debt • bait and switch • bankrupt • bankruptcy •bar •bar review course • basis • bench • best evidence rule • big gun •bilious •billable hour •birdie •black
ck letter law • blue book • bogart • bogie • boiler plate • bonus • book •boot •booty • bork •bribe • bust •busted • c.a.f.o. •calendar call • chain • child su
rning the file • circumstantial evidence •citation • class action • clearly • clients • closing costs • coffee • comparative negligence • compensatory dama
ideration • constitutional law • contract • contributory negligence • contumacious •corporation • corpus delicti • counselor • creditor • cross examination • dea
ad man's acts • deceit • deep pocket • de minimis non curat lex • demurrer • deposition • derogatory clause • devil's dictionary • dictionary, law • directed ve
closure • divorce • dormant commerce clause • dorr's Rebellion • double billing • double jeopardy • due process • dying declaration • e.s.o.p. employee share ow
plan • eagle • economic development program • ego • eighth amendment •ejuration • entitlement • equal protection clause • equity • escheat •estate • es
ppel, equitable • ethics • evidence, laws of / rules of • excited utterance • exclusionary rule • exculpatory evidence rule • exhaustion of remedies • ex-wif
and • face time • fair • fair use doctrine • fairway • false arrest • federal judge • federalism • federalism • federal witness protection program • federalist sc
h amendment • fifteenth amendment • filibuster • first amendment • floating crap game • fourteenth amendment • fourth amendment • force majeure • fra
ege •fraud • frivolous • fruit of the poisonous tree • fundamental right • garden • general denial • gerrymander • gift causa mortis • gift tax • gloss • good sa
, Learned • harmless error • harvard law • hassle • hazardous • hazardous waste • headnote • hearsay • heirloom • hereinabove, hereinafter, heretofore • he
aid • homicide • hornbook • hose • hundred weight • hung jury • ill fame • immoral • impediment to marriage • import-export clause • imputed negligence • imp
orporation by reference • income • inchoate • indemnity • indigent • inevitable discovery rule • infancy • internal Revenue code • internal Revenue service • imp
al property • interstate commerce • ipso facto • irrelevant • jack • jeopardy • judicial review • jump • jail • jailhouse lawyer • joint and several liability • journa
ege • judgment • judgment not withstanding the verdict • jurisprudence • jury • jury instructions • jury wheel • just compensation • justice • justification • k
iver-cellars act • kentucky rule • kick • kickback • kilo • kiting • kleptomania • knock and announce • know • know-it-all • known-heirs • laches, estoppel by •
act • lapse in judgement • law • law of the case • law review • lawyer's trust account • lead counsel • legislative intent • liability • libel • link • liquidated dam
jation • loaded • long-arm jurisdiction • lose • maintenance • malice aforethought • malicious prosecution • malpractice insurance • manual labor • making a r
rriage • matrone • mason • matlock, ben • maundering • mcnaughton Rule • mendacity • mens rea • merely • minnesota twins, the • monopoly • mortgage i
• multi-state • navigable waters • negligence • new york • new york lawyers • ninth amendment • no-knock warrant • not-for-profit corporation • nutshell • c
m • objection • obscenity • offer • old bailey • oligarchy • originalist • paternity • paternity test • palimony • penultimate • perspicuity • pike test • plea ba
ssey v. ferguson • potter, stewart • poverty law • pornography • prevarication • product liability • professional responsibility • prior inconsistent statement •
aint • profix • public interest law • public interest lawyer • punitive damages • quantum meruit • quash • quarter section • question presented • quid pro quo •
• deed • rainmaker • rational basis test • rejection • remand • residuum • residuum rule • res ipsa loquitor • res judicata • respondent superior • responsible o
• rule against perpetuities • screw • screw-the-pooch • second amendment • sentence • separation of powers • settlement • seventh amendment • sinking fu
enth amendment • sixth amendment • slander • solicitation • spendthrift • stare decisis • stages of marriage • statute • statutes of frauds • street lawyer •
ruction • strict scrutiny • sub rosa • substantive due process • sudden heat of passion • summer associate • taylor law • take it upstairs • taxation • tenth am
• think-they-know-it-all • third amendment • tickle • title insurance • tort • to wit • traduce • trespass • trust • ultimate • unambiguous • unconstitutional • uni
hercial code • unique • united states supreme court • unjust enrichment • usury • usufruct • vagrant • verified pleading • very • waiver • warhorse • warr
ss • warranty, implied • warranty period • ways-and-means • webster, daniel • west publishing • whole-life insurance • wirt, william • withholding • yield •
el • zealous representation • zone of interest test • zoning • absence of malice • accessory • accomplice • acquit • act of god • action • activist judge • actus
inistrative law • admiralty law • agent • albatross • alimony • alternative pleading • amnesty • ambulance chaser • antitrust laws • appeal • arbitrary •
el • armed and dangerous • as is • assumpsit • attorney • b.m.w. • bad debt • bait and switch • bankrupt • bankruptcy •bar •bar review course • basis • ber
evidence rule • big gun •bilious •billable hour •birdie •black acre • black letter law • blue book • bogart • bogie • boiler plate • bonus • book •boot •booty •
ie • bust •busted • c.a.f.o. •calendar call • chain • child support •churning the file • circumstantial evidence •citation • class action • clearly • clients • cl
• coffee • comparative negligence • compensatory damages • consideration • constitutional law • contract • contributory negligence • contumacious •cor
• corpus delicti • counselor • creditor • cross examination • dead file • dead man's acts • deceit • deep pocket • de minimis non curat lex • demurrer • depos
ogatory clause • devil's dictionary • dictionary, law • directed verdict • disclosure • divorce • dormant commerce clause • dorr's Rebellion • double billing • dc
rdy • due process • dying declaration • e.s.o.p. employee share ownership plan • eagle absence of malice • accessory • accomplice • acquit • act of god • a
vist judge • actus reus • administrative law • admiralty law • agent • albatross • alimony • alternative pleading • amnesty • ambulance chaser • antitrust la
al • arbitrary and capricious • armed and dangerous • as is • assumpsit • attorney • b.m.w. • bad debt • bait and switch • bankrupt • bankruptcy •bar •bar re
ie • basis • bench • best evidence rule • big gun •bilious •billable hour •birdie •black acre • black letter law • blue book • bogart • bogie • boiler plate • bon
•boot •booty • bork •bribe • bust •busted • c.a.f.o. •calendar call • chain • child support •churning the file • circumstantial evidence •citation • class acti
y • clients • closing costs • coffee • comparative negligence • compensatory damages • consideration • constitutional law • contract • contributory negligen
macious •corporation • corpus delicti • counselor • creditor • cross examination • dead file • dead man's acts • deceit • deep pocket • de minimis non cur
rrer • deposition • derogatory clause • devil's dictionary • dictionary, law • directed verdict • disclosure • divorce • dormant commerce clause • dorr's Rebelli
e billing • double jeopardy • due process • dying declaration • e.s.o.p. employee share ownership plan • eagle • economic development program • ego • ei
dment •ejuration • entitlement • equal protection clause • equity • escheat • estate • estop • estoppel, equitable • ethics • evidence, laws of / rules of • exe
ince • exclusionary rule • exculpatory evidence rule • exhaustion of remedies • ex-wife/ex-husband • face time • fair • fair use doctrine • fairway • false arre
al judge • federalism • federal witness protection program • federalist society • fifth amendment • filibuster • first amendment • floating crap game • fourte
dment • fourth amendment • force majeure • franking privilege •fraud • frivolous • fruit of the poisonous tree • fundamental right • garden • general denial • g
er • gift causa mortis • gift tax • gloss • good samaritan statues • got my papers! • great compromise • graft • gross • guarantee clause • guilt • h.a.p. • ha
s • habitability, habitability, warrantee of • hack • hand, Learned • harmless error • harvard law • hassle • hazardous • hazardous waste • headnote • hearsa

APPENDIX B:
Lawyers in Song

Lawyers have made many contributions to the great works of arts and letters. You won't find the following songs among those contributions. Still, songs and stories have always taken people's minds off their troubles and lifted their spirits. Even lawyers who love their jobs may become discouraged or disillusioned. Listening to some of these will lift your spirits when you think that maybe you should have gone to business school instead of law school. These are the top twelve lawyer songs, best to worst, based on my own subjective taste and peculiar sense of humor.

1. Appointed Forever

(The Bar and Grill Singers)

This parody of *For All My Life*—actually sung by lawyers—has clever lyrics that are completely on point. It also has great musical quality. The Bar and Grill Singers have at least three albums, all of which are worth owning, and most if their songs are "on point," as we lawyers like to say. Limiting them to one entry in the top twelve was the only way to achieve the diversity that makes our society vibrant and strong.

2. My Attorney Bernie

(Stan Frishberg)

Frishberg recounts all the reasons why he is in love with his attorney Bernie. Frishberg's light touch on the piano and fun lyrics will warm your heart after a bad day at the office. Most lawyers will want to be his attorney Bernie.

3. Lawyers, Guns, and Money

(Various Artists)

This Warren Zevon song has been on more lawyers' answering machines than the Gambini Crime family. It would have rated #1 except it is about a man who needs lawyers, guns, and money—not lawyers, guns, and money themselves.

Many singers—including Hank Williams, Jr., and Meatloaf—have covered this tune, but none surpass Zevon's renditions. Zevon's album *Learning to Flinch* includes an acoustic version that imparts a greater sense of desperation than his electric original.

4. Divorce Lawyers, Funeral Directors and Jailors

(Ferlin Husky)

All would-be lawyers should listen to this song before applying to law school. It will make them think about their future role as one of society's parasites. For the rest of us, it could lead to dangerous introspection—at least until the next six-digit retainer goes into the I.O.L.T.A.

5. Lawyer Clark Blues

(John Estes)

In 1941, John Estes recorded this song about an attorney he supposedly knew. In the song, lawyer Clark promises to keep him out of the pen. This is clearly a violation of several disciplinary rules in the code of professional conduct, and we are looking for lawyer Clark to attempt disbarment—if he is still alive.

6. Lawyers in Love

(Jackson Browne)

I have no idea what the lyrics are about, but Jackson Brown sounds great on a sultry summer night when you're racing down a country road in a '72 Pontiac on your way to meet an agreeable companion.

7. Here Comes the Judge

(Bobby Biggs)

This song contains the quintessential judge line, "Everybody's doin' time today."

8. Kill all Lawyers

(Kevin Andrews)

This song made the list because it includes a femme fatale that would speed the pulse of any red-blooded law student—male or female—albeit for different reasons.

9. One Million Lawyers

(Tom Paxton)

Being compared to epic natural disasters and notorious conquerors is rather flattering.

10. Samovar the Lawyer

(Dick Vosburgh and Frank Lazarus)

The award-winning play "A Day in Hollywood/A Night in the Ukraine" features a fine imitation of the Marx Brothers. This song is not as clever as "Lydia the Tattooed Lady," but it is the best lawyer song that Groucho never performed.

11. Lawyers Suck

(The Random Brothers)

This boisterous rousing anthem could have beer halls rocking in any blue-collar town. And hearing oneself compared unfavorably to snakes and viruses is always uplifting.

12. Mommy is a Lawyer

(Kenny Young and the Egg Plants)

This song consists of slow repetitive moaning that "Everyone is a lawyer." I heard it once on the radio years ago. It is one of those songs that has the detestable quality of lodging in your mind and, unbidden, playing itself over and over again. The C.I.A. could torture hardened terrorists into confessing everything they know just by playing this song before breakfast every morning at Guantanamo Bay. I listened to it again to be sure my report on it for this book would be accurate. Now I can truly say I've suffered for my art.

debt • bait and switch • bankrupt • bankruptcy •bar •bar review course • basis • bench • best evidence rule • big gun •bilious •billable hour •birdie •black a
k letter law • blue book • bogart • bogie • boiler plate • bonus • book •boot •booty • bork •bribe • bust • busted • c.a.f.o. •calendar call • chain • child sup
ing the file • circumstantial evidence •citation • class action • clearly • clients • closing costs • coffee • comparative negligence • compensatory damage
eration • constitutional law • contract • contributory negligence • contumacious •corporation • corpus delicti • counselor • creditor • cross examination • dead
d man's acts • deceit • deep pocket • de minimis non curat lex • demurrer • deposition • derogatory clause • devil's dictionary • dictionary, law • directed ver
osure • divorce • dormant commerce clause • dorr's Rebellion • double jeopardy • due process • dying declaration • e.s.o.p. employee share owni
lan • eagle • economic development program • ego • eighth amendment •ejuration • entitlement • equal protection clause • equity • escheat •estate • esto
hel, equitable • ethics • evidence, laws of / rules of • excited utterance • exclusionary rule • exculpatory evidence rule • exhaustion of remedies • ex-wife,
nd • face time • fair • fair use doctrine • fairway • false arrest • federal judge • federalism • federalism • federal witness protection program • federalist soc
amendment • fifteenth amendment • filibuster • first amendment • floating crap game • fourteenth amendment • fourth amendment • force majeure • fran
ge •fraud • frivolous • fruit of the poisonous tree • fundamental right • garden • general denial • gerrymander • gift causa mortis • gift tax • gloss • good sam
atues • got my papers! • great compromise • graft • gross • guarantee clause • guilt • h.a.p. • habeas corpus • habitability • habitability, warrantee of • hac
Learned • harmless error • harvard law • hassle • hazardous • hazardous waste • headnote • hearsay • heirloom • hereinabove, hereinafter, heretofore • he s
d • homicide • hornbook • hose • hundred weight • hung jury • ill fame • immoral • impediment to marriage • import-export clause • imputed negligence • impe
rporation by reference • income • inchoate • indemnity • indigent • inevitable discovery rule • infancy • internal Revenue code • internal Revenue service • in
property • interstate commerce • ipso facto • irrelevant • jack • jeopardy • judicial review • jump • jail • jailhouse lawyer • joint and several liability • journal
ge • judgment • judgment not withstanding the verdict • jurisprudence • jury • jury instructions • jury wheel • just compensation • justice • justification • k.
er-cellars act • kentucky rule • kick • kickback • kilo • kiting • kleptomania • knock and announce • know • know-it-all • known-heirs • laches, estoppel by •
ict • lapse in judgement • law • law of the case • law review • lawyer's trust account • lead counsel • legislative intent • liability • libel • link • liquidated dama
ation • loaded • long-arm jurisdiction • lose • maintenance • malice aforethought • malicious prosecution • malpractice insurance • manual labor • making a rec
iage • marrone • mason • matlock, ben • maundering • mcnaughton Rule • mendacity • mens rea • merely • minnesota twins, the • monopoly • mortgage in
multi-state • navigable waters • negligence • new york • new york lawyers • ninth amendment • no-knock warrant • not-for-profit corporation • nutshell • ob
a • objection • obscenity • offer • old bailey • oligarchy • originalist • paternity • paternity test • palimony • penultimate • perspicuity • pike test • plea barg
sey v. ferguson • potter, stewart • poverty law • pornography • prevarication • product liability • professional responsibility • prior inconsistent statement • p
nt • prolix • public interest law • public interest lawyer • punitive damages • quantum meruit • quash • quarter section • question presented • quid pro quo • c
deed • rainmaker • rational basis test • rejection • remand • residuum • residuum rule • res ipsa loquitor • res judicata • respondent superior • responsible off
rule against perpetuities • screw • screw-the-pouch • second amendment • sentence • separation of powers • settlement • seventh amendment • sinking fun
ith amendment • sixth amendment • slander • solicitation • spendthrift • stare decisis • stages of marriage • statute • statutes of frauds • street lawyer • s
ruction • strict scrutiny • sub rosa • substantive due process • sudden heat of passion • summer associate • taylor law • take it upstairs • taxation • tenth ame
think-they-know-it-all • third amendment • tickle • title insurance • tort • to wit • traduce • trespass • trust • ultimate • unambiguous • unconstitutional • unif
ercial code • unique • united states supreme court • unjust enrichment • usury • usufruct • vagrant • verified pleading • very • waiver • warhorse • warra
s • warranty, implied • warranty period • ways-and-means • webster, daniel • west publishing • whole-life insurance • writ, william • withholding • yield • y
l • zealous representation • zone of interest test • zoning • absence of malice • accessory • accomplice • acquit • act of god • action • activist judge • actus r
inistrative law • admiralty law • agent • albatross • alimony • alternative pleading • amnesty • ambulance chaser • antitrust laws • appeal • arbitrary and ca
• armed and dangerous • as is • assumpsit • attorney • b.m.w. • bad debt • bait and switch • bankrupt • bankruptcy •bar •bar review course • basis • benc
vidence rule • big gun •bilious •billable hour •birdie •black acre • black letter law • blue book • bogart • bogie • boiler plate • bonus • book •boot •booty • b
• bust •busted • c.a.f.o. •calendar call • chain • child support •churning the file • circumstantial evidence •citation • class action • clearly • clients • clos
• coffee • comparative negligence • compensatory damages • consideration • constitutional law • contract • contributory negligence • contumacious •corp
corpus delicti • counselor • creditor • cross examination • dead file • dead man's acts • deceit • deep pocket • de minimis non curat lex • demurrer • depositi
gatory clause • devil's dictionary • dictionary, law • directed verdict • disclosure • divorce • dormant commerce clause • dorr's Rebellion • double billing • do
dy • due process • dying declaration • e.s.o.p. employee share ownership plan • eagle absence of malice • accessory • accomplice • acquit • act of god • act
ist judge • actus reus • administrative law • admiralty law • agent • albatross • alimony • alternative pleading • amnesty • ambulance chaser • antitrust law
• arbitrary and capricious • armed and dangerous • as is • assumpsit • attorney • b.m.w. • bad debt • bait and switch • bankrupt • bankruptcy •bar •bar rev
• basis • bench • best evidence rule • big gun •bilious •billable hour •birdie •black acre • black letter law • blue book • bogart • bogie • boiler plate • bonu
boot •booty • bork •bribe • bust •busted • c.a.f.o. •calendar call • chain • child support •churning the file • circumstantial evidence •citation • class actio
• clients • closing costs • coffee • comparative negligence • compensatory damages • consideration • constitutional law • contract • contributory negligenc
acious •corporation • corpus delicti • counselor • creditor • cross examination • dead file • dead man's acts • deceit • deep pocket • de minimis non curat la
• deposition • derogatory clause • devil's dictionary • dictionary, law • directed verdict • disclosure • divorce • dormant commerce clause • dorr's Rebellic
billing • double jeopardy • due process • dying declaration • e.s.o.p. employee share ownership plan • eagle • economic development program • ego • eig
ment •ejuration • entitlement • equal protection clause • equity • escheat •estate • estop • estoppel, equitable • ethics • evidence, laws of / rules of • exc
nce • exclusionary rule • exculpatory evidence rule • exhaustion of remedies • ex-wife/ex-husband • face time • fair • fair use doctrine • fairway • false arres
l judge • federalism • federal witness protection program • federalist society • fifth amendment • filibuster • first amendment • floating crap game • fourte
ment • fourth amendment • force majeure • franking privilege •fraud • frivolous • fruit of the poisonous tree • fundamental right • garden • general denial • ge
r • gift causa mortis • gift tax • gloss • good samaritan statues • got my papers! • great compromise • graft • gross • guarantee clause • guilt • h.a.p. • hab
• habitability • habitability, warrantee of • hack • hand, Learned • harmless error • harvard law • hassle • hazardous • hazardous waste • headnote • hearso

APPENDIX C:
A Directory of Preeminent Firms

dictionary of legal bullshit

Able and Goodmen Attorneys At Law
Military Justice
Veterans Benefits

Abbey, Parish, Kirk and Priest
Representing Religious
Organizations Worldwide

Aims and Schutz Firearms Law
Licenses, Permits,
Ownership

Archer, Hunter, and Fisher
Specialists in
Natural Resource Damages

Bates and Switch, P.C.
Over 100 Associates to serve
your needs
Free initial consultations with
our respected partners
www.churnthecases.law

Black, White and Brown
Civil Rights, Equal Access, &
Section 1983 Litigation

Bones, Hurt & Aiken
Specialists in Workers'
Compensation
Repetitive Motion
Back and Neck Injuries

Boot, Ralph, Euker, Hurely and Spitz
D.W.I. & Controlled
Substances

Boss, Diels, & Fuks, P.C.
Paternity
Sexual Harassment
Wrongful Discharge
www.wegetsome.com

Buggs & Shafts
Collections

Burrows, Sands, Stone, Cole, & Clay, P.L.L.C.
Mineral Rights and Mining
Law Specialists

Cage and Caine
Attorneys At Law
Criminal Defense &
Prisoners' Rights

Chaffe and Burns, P.C.
"We're on your case"

Carpenter and Mason
Your Labor Lawyers

Carter, Porter and Wheeler
Specialists in
Transportation Law

**Cook, Lamb, Burger, &
Hamm**
Advocates for Animal Rights

**Cooper, Caulker,
Shoemaker, and Smith**
Experts in unemployment
claims since 1938

**Cox, Goetz, Bush & Klimpt
Attorneys at Law**
Divorce, Custody & Paternity

Cross, Palm and Wink
Criminal Defense Lawyers

Daye & Knight, P.L.L.C.
300 associates
to serve your needs

DeBeers and Schotz, P.L.L.C.
D.U.I.
Dramshop Liability
Liquor Licenses

**DeGasse, Chambers, Gallo,
and Graves, P.C.**
A law practice focused on
criminal appeals

Diggs, Pitts, and Saltz, P.C.
Securing claims and mineral
rights for landowners and
industry

Drinker and Driver
Attorneys at Law
Harvey Drinker, Esq.

**Evan, Steven, and Glad,
P.L.L.C.**
Contracts
Remedies
Uniform Commercial Code

Farmer, Plant, Field & Grow
Attorneys at Law
Crop Insurance
Bankruptcy

**Finger, Bogart, Filch, Nick,
and Steele, P.L.L.C.**
Experienced Criminal
Attorneys

Fish Deere Fox & O'Hare
Attorneys specializing in
environmental law

183

dictionary of legal bullshit

Fixx, Bunco, and Rico, P.C.
Experts in Risk Management
and Insurance Claims

Flay and Pound, P.C.
Collections & Civil Recoveries

Gamble and Luz
Attorneys at Law
Representing Gaming
Establishments

Gayle, Schols, & Strand, P.C.
Admiralty Law, Maritime Law

Greasey, Sheen, and Drum, P.C.
Environmental Lawyers
specializing in Superfund and
Toxic Tort Defense

Green, Parr, and Flagg, P.C.
Attorneys and Agents
Sports Law and
Representation

Haak & Luger
Tobacco Litigation

Hammer and Screw
Tort, Matrimonial, and
Bankruptcy

Hatchet, Jobs, and Bull
Litigators
Noah Bull, Esq., Senior
Partner

Haus and Holmes
Attorneys at Law
Real Estate & Bankruptcy

Hiram & Winn
Attorneys Specializing in
Celebrity Criminal Defense

Izzi, Wright, Ore, Knot, & Co.
Discrete Private
Investigations
Divorce, Embezzlement,
Fraud, and Prenuptial
Assurance

Joy & Hope
Attorneys at Law
Your Adoption Specialists

The Kant-Barrett Law Firm
Employment Relations:
Age Discrimination, Sexual
Harassment, and Intentional
Infliction of Emotional
Distress

Karp and Moen
Attorneys at Law
Prisoners' Rights
Public Interest Litigation

Lay, Lowe, and Waite
Feds want you to roll over?
RICO, conspiracy, or bribery
charges?
Call us now!

Lear & Long
Attorneys At Law
Specializing in Sexual
Harassment

Leary & Fabian, P.L.L.C.
Contract & Transactional Law

Locke & Key
Attorneys at Law
Specializing in
Criminal Appeals

March and Blair
Lawyers with a social
conscience

**Marsh, Rivers, Lake
and Woods, P.C**
Natural Resource Law

**Mills, Stack, Belcher
Ashe & Moore, P.L.L.C.**
Title V, P.S.D., and NSPS, &
NESHAP

Odessa — Gudenov
Counselors at Law
Public Assistance
Tenants' Rights
Administrative Claims

**Paige, Paige, McCall and
Mailer**
Telecommunications Law

Palm, Coyne & Skate
Bail Bonds

**Parras, London, Rome &
Washington, P.C.**
Attorneys and Counselors
serving clients in a
transnational market

**Pelt, Trapper, Skinner,
Tanner & Hyde**
Serving the fashion and
garment industries since
2007 B.C.

Pine & Howell
Attorneys at Law
Divorce, Custody, Paternity,
Parental Rights

Poke & Pryor, LLP
Private Investigations

Potts, Blow, Coker, & Tripper
Attorneys at Law
Narcotics Defense
Asset Forfeitures
Federal Sentencing
Guidelines

**The Law Offices of
Punch, Chad, and Blair**
Election Law

Quibbel & Becker
Mediation and Arbitration

**Raine, Hale, Snow & Eiss
Attorneys at Law**
Contract Law
Performance Disputes
Remedies

**Random Samples and
Poole**
Assisting Lawyers with
Polling, Focus Groups,
& Jury Profiles

Ray—Gunn, P.L.L.C.
Intellectual Property
Government Procurement

**Rhodes, Bridges, Barnes,
and Holmes**
Construction Law
& Land Use Planning

Sharpe and Whittier
Attorneys & Registered
Lobbyists
Procurement
Administrative Procedures

Slaughter, English & Babble
Counselors at Law
Specializing in Appellate
Litigation

Small and Petty
Attorneys at Law
Divorce, Child Custody,
Child Support, Prenuptial
Agreements

Stahl, Delay & Waite
Pretrial Litigation Experts
Fee Sharing

**Street, Walker, & Hooker,
P.L.L.C.**
A law firm representing
entrepreneurs

**Tidewater, Lighter,
Briggs & Oar**
Specialists in Admiralty Law

Till, Field, and Plant, P.C.
Lawyers Serving
Agri-Business

**Tooms and Graves,
Attorneys**
Wills, Probate and
Estate Planning

Tripp and Soo, A Law Firm
Personal Injury
Product Liability
Class Action
Emotional Distress

**Truax, Block, Gallo, & Gunn,
P.C.**
Criminal Law, Capital Appeals

**Vig, Costas, Moore &
Moore, P.C.**
Banking, Finance,
& Securities Law

Wade, Rivers & Hyde
A Law Firm
Immigration & Naturalization

William I. Welsh, Esq.
Bankruptcy Law
Capitol Street

Wise, Guy & Whacker
Attorneys
Representing a Select
Clientele
New Clients by Referral Only

Wright and Tinker, P.L.L.C.
Intellectual Property Law

Yak & Yak
Mediation and Arbitration

Zonne & Aut
LSAT Preparation
through Lectures,
Practice Tests,
and
Rigorous Memorization

debt • bait and switch • bankrupt • bankruptcy •bar •bar review course • basis • bench • best evidence rule • big gun •bilious •billable hour •birdie •black
k letter law • blue book • bogart • bogie • boiler plate • bonus • book •boot •booty • bork •bribe • bust •busted • c.a.f.o. •calendar call • chain • child sup
ning the file • circumstantial evidence •citation • class action • clearly • clients • closing costs • coffee • comparative negligence • compensatory damag
deration • constitutional law • contract • contributory negligence • contumacious •corporation • corpus delicti • counselor • creditor • cross examination • dead
d man's acts • deceit • deep pocket • de minimis non curat lex • demurrer • deposition • derogatory clause • devil's dictionary • dictionary, law • directed ve
losure • divorce • dormant commerce clause • dorr's Rebellion • double billing • double jeopardy • due process • dying declaration • e.s.o.p. employee share ow
lan • eagle • economic development program • ego • eighth amendment •ejuration • entitlement • equal protection clause • equity • escheat •estate • este
bel, equitable • ethics • evidence, laws of / rules of • excited utterance • exclusionary rule • exculpatory evidence rule • exhaustion of remedies • ex-wife
nd • face time • fair • fair use doctrine • fairway • false arrest • federal judge • federalism • federalism • federal witness protection program • federalist soc
amendment • fifteenth amendment • filibuster • first amendment • floating crap game • fourteenth amendment • fourth amendment • force majeure • fran
ge •fraud • frivolous • fruit of the poisonous tree • fundamental right • garden • general denial • gerrymander • gift causa mortis • gift tax • gloss • good sa
atues • got my papers! • great compromise • graft • gross • guarantee clause • guilt • h.a.p. • habeas corpus • habitability • habitability, warrantee of • ha
Learned • harmless error • harvard law • hassle • hazardous • hazardous waste • headnote • hearsay • heirloom • hereinabove, hereinafter, heretofore • he s
id • homicide • hornbook • hose • hundred weight • hung jury • ill fame • immoral • impediment to marriage • import-export clause • imputed negligence • impe
rporation by reference • income • inchoate • indemnity • indigent • inevitable discovery rule • infancy • internal Revenue code • internal Revenue service • in
l property • interstate commerce • ipso facto • irrelevant • jack • jeopardy • judicial review • jump • jail • jailhouse lawyer • joint and several liability • journa
ge • judgment • judgment not withstanding the verdict • jurisprudence • jury • jury instructions • jury wheel • just compensation • justice • justification • k
ver-cellars act • kentucky rule • kick • kickback • kilo • kiting • kleptomania • knock and announce • know • know-it-all • known-heirs • laches, estoppel by •
ct • lapse in judgement • law • law of the case • law review • lawyer's trust account • lead counsel • legislative intent • liability • libel • link • liquidated dama
ation • loaded • long-arm jurisdiction • lose • maintenance • malice aforethought • malicious prosecution • malpractice insurance • manual labor • making a re
riage • marrone • mason • matlock, ben • maundering • mcnaughton Rule • mendacity • mens rea • merely • minnesota twins, the • monopoly • mortgage in
• multi-state • navigable waters • negligence • new york • new york lawyers • ninth amendment • no-knock warrant • not-for-profit corporation • nutshell • ol
n • objection • obscenity • offer • old bailey • oligarchy • originalist • paternity • paternity test • palimony • penultimate • perspicuity • pike test • plea bar
sey v. ferguson • potter, stewart • poverty law • pornography • prevarication • product liability • professional responsibility • prior inconsistent statement •
int • prolix • public interest law • public interest lawyer • punitive damages • quantum meruit • quash • quarter section • question presented • quid pro quo •
deed • rainmaker • rational basis test • rejection • remand • residuum • residuum rule • res ipsa loquitor • res judicata • respondent superior • responsible of
rule against perpetuities • screw • screw-the-pooch • second amendment • sentence • separation of powers • settlement • seventh amendment • sinking fun
nth amendment • sixth amendment • slander • solicitation • spendthrift • stare decisis • stages of marriage • statute • statutes of frauds • street lawyer • si
uction • strict scrutiny • sub rosa • substantive due process • sudden heat of passion • summer associate • taylor law • take it upstairs • taxation • tenth am
• think-they-know-it-all • third amendment • tickle • title insurance • tort • to wit • traduce • trespass • trust • ultimate • unambiguous • unconstitutional • unif
ercial code • unique • united states supreme court • unjust enrichment • usury • usufruct • vagrant • verified pleading • very • waiver • warhorse • warra
ss • warranty, implied • warranty period • ways-and-means • webster, daniel • west publishing • whole-life insurance • witt, william • withholding • yield • y
al • zealous representation • zone of interest test • zoning • absence of malice • accessory • accomplice • acquit • act of god • activist judge • actus
inistrative law • admiralty law • agent • albatross • alimony • alternative pleading • amnesty • ambulance chaser • antitrust laws • appeal • arbitrary and ca
• armed and dangerous • as is • assumpsit • attorney • b.m.w. • bad debt • bait and switch • bankrupt • bankruptcy •bar •bar review course • basis • ben
vidence rule • big gun •bilious •billable hour •birdie •black acre • black letter law • blue book • bogart • bogie • boiler plate • bonus • book •boot •booty •
• • bust •busted • c.a.f.o. •calendar call • chain • child support •churning the file • circumstantial evidence •citation • class action • clearly • clients • clo
• coffee • comparative negligence • compensatory damages • consideration • constitutional law • contract • contributory negligence • contumacious •corp
corpus delicti • counselor • creditor • cross examination • dead file • dead man's acts • deceit • deep pocket • de minimis non curat lex • demurrer • deposi
gatory clause • devil's dictionary • dictionary, law • directed verdict • disclosure • divorce • dormant commerce clause • dorr's Rebellion • double billing • do
dy • due process • dying declaration • e.s.o.p. employee share ownership plan • eagle absence of malice • accessory • accomplice • acquit • act of god • ac
vist judge • actus reus • administrative law • admiralty law • agent • albatross • alimony • alternative pleading • amnesty • ambulance chaser • antitrust law
• • arbitrary and capricious • armed and dangerous • as is • assumpsit • attorney • b.m.w. • bad debt • bait and switch • bankrupt • bankruptcy •bar •bar
• basis • bench • best evidence rule • big gun •bilious •billable hour •birdie •black acre • black letter law • blue book • bogart • bogie • boiler plate • bon
•boot •booty • bork •bribe • bust •busted • c.a.f.o. •calendar call • chain • child support •churning the file • circumstantial evidence •citation • class actio
• clients • closing costs • coffee • comparative negligence • compensatory damages • consideration • constitutional law • contract • contributory negligenc
nacious •corporation • corpus delicti • counselor • creditor • cross examination • dead file • dead man's acts • deceit • deep pocket • de minimis non curat l
rer • deposition • derogatory clause • devil's dictionary • dictionary, law • directed verdict • disclosure • divorce • dormant commerce clause • dorr's Rebelli
• billing • double jeopardy • due process • dying declaration • e.s.o.p. employee share ownership plan • eagle • economic development program • ego • eig
ment •ejuration • entitlement • equal protection clause • equity • escheat •estate • estop • estoppel, equitable • ethics • evidence, laws of / rules of • exc
nce • exclusionary rule • exculpatory evidence rule • exhaustion of remedies • ex-wife/ex-husband • face time • fair • fair use doctrine • fairway • false arre
l judge • federalism • federal witness protection program • federalist society • fifth amendment • filibuster • first amendment • floating crap game • fourtee
ment • fourth amendment • force majeure • franking privilege •fraud • frivolous • fruit of the poisonous tree • fundamental right • garden • general denial • ge
• • gift causa mortis • gift tax • gloss • good samaritan statues • got my papers! • great compromise • graft • gross • guarantee clause • guilt • h.a.p. • h
• habitability • habitability, warrantee of • hack • hand, Learned • harmless error • harvard law • hassle • hazardous • hazardous waste • headnote • hearsa
• hereinabove, hereinafter, heretofore • he said, she said • homicide • hornbook • hose • hundred weight • hung jury • ill fame

DISCLAIMER

In case you haven't noticed, this is a work of satire. Do not rely on any part of this book as legal authority for any argument you want people to take seriously. People don't pay attention to what the author writes even when he works desperately to persuade people of his gravitas—so for the sake of your reputation, put the contents of this book out of your mind after you read it.

The names, addresses, and telephone numbers herein are fictitious. They were made up strictly for entertainment value. Any resemblance to actual persons, firms, or other entities is strictly coincidence or the result of an innate human desire to find order in the frightening chaos of the world. If the name of your law firm really is "Haak and Luger," please add a couple of new partners to the letterhead.

No animals were harmed in the making of this book—except one big hairy spider that crawled out from under the keyboard about midnight as the author was about to take a sip of scalding hot tea. Although the spider died, his suffering was brief compared to the author, who spent a week walking as if he'd just finished a 1,000-mile cattle drive. Also—in the interest of full disclosure—a calico cat was repeatedly moved from the author's desk to the floor, but she seemed to find this entertaining.

The contents are not to be taken internally. If swallowed, do not induce vomiting. Call a health care professional with good malpractice insurance because he'll probably screw up and leave you a debilitated, pain-wracked invalid for decades to come.

The contents are inflammable, if not inflammatory. Keep away from open flame and direct heat sources and any dolts who take everything seriously. Not to be used as a floatation device in the event of a water landing. Choking hazard. Keep away from children under 21, compulsive eaters, nail biters, and law professors. Use extreme care in handling pages, as the edges can cause paper cuts, which can be really painful boo-boos.

If the voices in your head still manage to convince you that this book is to blame for your problems, you should know that the author is broke. See judgment proof hereinabove. See also, "hereinabove" hereinabove.

d debt • bait and switch • bankrupt • bankruptcy •bar •bar review course • basis • bench • best evidence rule • big gun •bilious •billable hour •birdie •black
ack letter law • blue book • bogart • bogie • boiler plate • bonus • book •boot •booty • bork •bribe • bust • busted • c.a.f.o. •calendar call • chain • child su
rning the file • circumstantial evidence •citation • class action • clearly • clients • closing costs • coffee • comparative negligence • compensatory dama
ideration • constitutional law • contract • contributory negligence • contumacious •corporation • corpus delicti • counselor • creditor • cross examination • dea
ad man's acts • deceit • deep pocket • de minimis non curat lex • demurrer • deposition • derogatory clause • devil's dictionary • dictionary, law • directed v
iclosure • divorce • dormant commerce clause • dorr's Rebellion • double billing • double jeopardy • due process • dying declaration • e.s.o.p. employee share ow
plan • eagle • economic development program • ego • eighth amendment •ejuration • entitlement • equal protection clause • equity • escheat •estate • es
opel, equitable • ethics • evidence, laws of / rules of • excited utterance • exclusionary rule • exculpatory evidence rule • exhaustion of remedies • ex-wi
and • face time • fair • fair use doctrine • fairway • false arrest • federal judge • federalism • federalism • federal witness protection program • federalist so
h amendment • fifteenth amendment • filibuster • first amendment • floating crap game • fourteenth amendment • fourth amendment • force majeure • fra
ege •fraud • frivolous • fruit of the poisonous tree • fundamental right • garden • general denial • gerrymander • gift causa mortis • gift tax • gloss • good sa
statutes • got my papers! • great compromise • graft • gross • guarantee clause • guilt • h.a.p. • habeas corpus • habitability • habitability, warrantee of • h
, Learned • harmless error • harvard law • hassle • hazardous • hazardous waste • headnote • hearsay • heirloom • hereinabove, hereinafter, heretofore •
aid • homicide • hornbook • hose • hundred weight • hung jury • ill fame • immoral • impediment to marriage • import-export clause • imputed negligence • imp
orporation by reference • income • inchoate • indemnity • indigent • inevitable discovery rule • infancy • internal Revenue code • internal Revenue service •
al property • interstate commerce • ipso facto • irrelevant • jack • jeopardy • judicial review • jump • jail • jailhouse lawyer • joint and several liability • journa
ege • judgment • judgment not withstanding the verdict • jurisprudence • jury • jury instructions • jury wheel • just compensation • justice • justification • k
ver-collars act • kentucky rule • kick • kickback • kilo • kiting • kleptomania • knock and announce • know • know-it-all • known-heirs • laches, estoppel by
act • lapse in judgement • law • law of the case • law review • lawyer's trust account • lead counsel • legislative intent • liability • libel • link • liquidated dan
gation • loaded • long-arm jurisdiction • lose • maintenance • malice aforethought • malicious prosecution • malpractice insurance • manual labor • making a re
rriage • marrone • mason • matlock, ben • maundering • mcnaughton Rule • mendacity • mens rea • merely • minnesota twins, the • monopoly • mortgage
• multi-state • navigable waters • negligence • new york • new york lawyers • ninth amendment • no-knock warrant • not-for-profit corporation • nutshell • c
m • objection • obscenity • offer • old bailey • oligarchy • originalist • paternity • paternity test • palimony • penultimate • perspicuity • pike test • plea ha
ssey v. ferguson • potter, stewart • poverty law • pornography • prevarication • product liability • professional responsibility • prior inconsistent statement •
oint • prolix • public interest law • public interest lawyer • punitive damages • quantum meruit • quash • quarter section • question presented • quid pro quo •
a deed • rainmaker • rational basis test • rejection • remand • residuum • residuum rule • res ipsa loquitor • res judicata • respondent superior • responsible o
 rule against perpetuities • screw • screw-the-pooch • second amendment • sentence • separation of powers • settlement • seventh amendment • sinking fo
enth amendment • sixth amendment • slander • solicitation • spendthrift • stare decisis • stages of marriage • statute • statutes of frauds • street lawyer •
truction • strict scrutiny • sub rosa • substantive due process • sudden heat of passion • summer associate • taylor law • take it upstairs • taxation • tenth ar
• think-they-know-it-all • third amendment • tickle • title insurance • tort • to wit • traduce • trespass • trust • ultimate • unambiguous • unconstitutional • un
nercial code • unique • united states supreme court • unjust enrichment • usury • usufruct • vagrant • verified pleading • very • waiver • warhorse • war
ess • warranty, implied • warranty period • ways-and-means • webster, daniel • west publishing • whole-life insurance • wirt, william • withholding • yield •
sel • zealous representation • zone of interest test • zoning • absence of malice • accessory • accomplice • acquit • act of god • action • activist judge • actus
ministrative law • admiralty law • agent • albatross • alimony • alternative pleading • amnesty • ambulance chaser • antitrust laws • appeal • arbitrary and c
s • armed and dangerous • as is • assumpsit • attorney • b.m.w. • bad debt • bait and switch • bankrupt • bankruptcy • bar •bar review course • basis • ben
evidence rule • big gun •bilious •billable hour •birdie •black acre • black letter law • blue book • bogart • bogie • boiler plate • bonus • bonk •boot •bonty •
e • bust •busted • c.a.f.o. •calendar call • chain • child support •churning the file • circumstantial evidence •citation • class action • clearly • clients • cl
s • coffee • comparative negligence • compensatorfy damages • consideration • constitutional law • contract • contributory negligence • contumacious •cor
corpus delicti • counselor • creditor • cross examination • dead file • dead man's acts • deceit • deep pocket • de minimis non curat lex • demurrer • depo
ogatory clause • devil's dictionary • dictionary, law • directed verdict • disclosure • divorce • dormant commerce clause • dorr's Rebellion • double billing • d
ardy • due process • dying declaration • e.s.o.p. employee share ownership plan • eagle absence of malice • accessory • accomplice • acquit • act of god • a
ivist judge • actus reus • administrative law • admiralty law • agent • albatross • alimony • alternative pleading • amnesty • ambulance chaser • antitrust la
al • arbitrary and capricious • armed and dangerous • as is • assumpsit • attorney • b.m.w. • bad debt • bait and switch • bankrupt • bankruptcy •bar •bar re
se • basis • bench • best evidence rule • big gun •bilious •billable hour •birdie •black acre • black letter law • blue book • bogart • bogie • boiler plate • bor
•boot •booty • bork •bribe • bust •busted • c.a.f.o. •calendar call • chain • child support •churning the file • circumstantial evidence •citation • class act
ly • clients • closing costs • coffee • comparative negligence • compensatory damages • consideration • constitutional law • contract • contributory negliger
umacious •corporation • corpus delicti • counselor • creditor • cross examination • dead file • dead man's acts • deceit • deep pocket • de minimis non curat
rrer • deposition • derogatory clause • devil's dictionary • dictionary, law • directed verdict • disclosure • divorce • dormant commerce clause • dorr's Rebell
le billing • double jeopardy • due process • dying declaration • e.s.o.p employee share ownership plan • eagle • economic development program • ego • e
ndment •ejuration • entitlement • equal protection clause • equity • escheat •estate • estop • estoppel, equitable • ethics • evidence, laws of / rules of • ex
ance • exclusionary rule • exculpatory evidence rule • exhaustion of remedies • ex-wife/ex-husband • face time • fair • fair use doctrine • fairway • false arr
al judge • federalism • federal witness protection program • federalist society • fifth amendment • filibuster • first amendment • floating crap game • fourte
dment • fourth amendment • force majeure • franking privilege •fraud • frivolous • fruit of the poisonous tree • fundamental right • garden • general denial • g
ler • gift causa mortis • gift tax • gloss • good samaritan statues • got my papers! • great compromise • graft • gross • guarantee clause • guilt • h.a.p. • ha
er • habitability, habitability, warrantee of • hack • hand, Learned • harmless error • harvard law • hassle • hazardous • hazardous waste • headnote • hear

ABOUT THE AUTHOR

Randall C. Young is an attorney and writer. He and his saintly wife, Patricia, have two children, Holly and Emmett, and a one-time stray calico cat that he was too soft-hearted to shoo away.

debt • bait and switch • bankrupt • bankruptcy • bar • bar review course • basis • bench • best evidence rule • big gun • bilious • billable hour • birdie • black
ack letter law • blue book • bogart • bogie • boiler plate • bonus • book • boot • booty • bork • bribe • bust • busted • c.a.f.o. • calendar call • chain • child s
urning the file • circumstantial evidence • citation • class action • clearly • clients • closing costs • coffee • comparative negligence • compensatory dama
sideration • constitutional law • contract • contributory negligence • contumacious • corporation • counselor • creditor • cross examination • de
ad man's acts • deceit • deep pocket • de minimis non curat lex • demurrer • deposition • derogatory clause • devil's dictionary • dictionary, law • directed v
sclosure • divorce • dormant commerce clause • dorr's Rebellion • double billing • double jeopardy • due process • dying declaration • e.s o p. employee share o
plan • eagle • economic development program • ego • eighth amendment • ejuration • entitlement • equal protection clause • equity • escheat • estate • es
ppel, equitable • ethics • evidence, laws of / rules of • excited utterance • exclusionary rule • exculpatory evidence rule • exhaustion of remedies • ex-wi
hand • face time • fair • fair use doctrine • fairway • false arrest • federal judge • federalism • federalism • federal witness protection program • federalist s
th amendment • fifteenth amendment • filibuster • first amendment • floating crap game • fourteenth amendment • fourth amendment • force majeure • fre
lege • fraud • frivolous • fruit of the poisonous tree • fundamental right • garden • general denial • gerrymander • gift causa mortis • gift tax • gloss • good s
statues • got my papers! • great compromise • graft • gross • guarantee clause • guilt • h.a.p. • habeas corpus • habitability • habitability, warrantee of • l
d, Learned • harmless error • harvard law • hassle • hazardous • hazardous waste • headnote • hearsay • heirloom • hereinabove, hereinafter, heretofore • he
said • homicide • hornbook • hose • hundred weight • hung jury • ill fame • immoral • impediment to marriage • import-export clause • imputed negligence • im
corporation by reference • income • inchoate • indemnity • indigent • inevitable discovery rule • infancy • internal Revenue code • internal Revenue service •
ial property • interstate commerce • ipso facto • irrelevant • jack • jeopardy • judicial review • jump • jail • jailhouse lawyer • joint and several liability • journ
lege • judgment • judgment not withstanding the verdict • jurisprudence • jury • jury instructions • jury wheel • just compensation • justice • justification • j
uver-cellars act • kentucky rule • kick • kickback • kilo • kiting • kleptomania • knock and announce • know • know-it-all • known-heirs • laches, estoppel by •
ract • lapse in judgement • law • law of the case • law review • lawyer's trust account • lead counsel • legislative intent • liability • libel • link • liquidated dan
gation • loaded • long-arm jurisdiction • lose • maintenance • malice aforethought • malicious prosecution • malpractice insurance • manual labor • making a
arriage • marrone • mason • matlock, ben • maundering • mcnaughton Rule • mendacity • mens rea • merely • minnesota twins, the • monopoly • mortgage
• multi-state • navigable waters • negligence • new york • new york lawyers • ninth amendment • no-knock warrant • not-for-profit corporation • nutshell
um • objection • obscenity • offer • old bailey • oligarchy • originalist • paternity • paternity test • palimony • penultimate • perspicuity • pike test • plea b
essey v ferguson • potter, stewart • poverty law • pornography • prevarication • product liability • professional responsibility • prior inconsistent statement •
raint • prolix • public interest law • public interest lawyer • punitive damages • quantum meruit • quash • quarter section • question presented • quid pro quo •
in deed • rainmaker • rational basis test • rejection • remand • residuum • residuum rule • res ipsa loquitor • res judicata • respondent superior • responsible
• rule against perpetuities • screw • screw-the-pooch • second amendment • sentence • separation of powers • settlement • seventh amendment • sinking
eenth amendment • sixth amendment • slander • solicitation • spendthrift • stare decisis • stages of marriage • statute • statutes of frauds • street lawyer
struction • strict scrutiny • sub rosa • substantive due process • sudden heat of passion • summer associate • taylor law • take it upstairs • taxation • tenth a
t • think-they-know-it-all • third amendment • tickle • title insurance • tort • to wit • traduce • trespass • trust • ultimate • unambiguous • unconstitutional • un
mercial code • unique • united states supreme court • unjust enrichment • usury • usufruct • vagrant • verified pleading • very • waiver • warhorse • wa
ess • warranty, implied • warranty period • ways-and-means • webster, daniel • west publishing • whole-life insurance • wirt, william • withholding • yield •
kel • zealous representation • zone of interest test • zoning • absence of malice • accessory • accomplice • acquit • act of god • action • activist judge • actu
ministrative law • admiralty law • agent • albatross • alimony • alternative pleading • amnesty • ambulance chaser • antitrust laws • appeal • arbitrary and
s • armed and dangerous • as is • assumpsit • attorney • b.m.w. • bad debt • bait and switch • bankrupt • bankruptcy • bar • bar review course • basis • be
evidence rule • big gun • bilious • billable hour • birdie • black acre • black letter law • blue book • bogart • bogie • boiler plate • bonus • book • boot • booty
be • bust • busted • c.a f.o. • calendar call • chain • child support • churning the file • circumstantial evidence • citation • class action • clearly • clients • c
s • coffee • comparative negligence • compensatorfy damages • consideration • constitutional law • contract • contributory negligence • contumacious • co
• corpus delicti • counselor • creditor • cross examination • dead file • dead man's acts • deceit • deep pocket • de minimis non curat lex • demurrer • depo
rogatory clause • devil's dictionary • dictionary, law • directed verdict • disclosure • divorce • dormant commerce clause • dorr's Rebellion • double billing • c
ardy • due process • dying declaration • e.s.o.p. employee share ownership plan • eagle absence of malice • accessory • accomplice • acquit • act of god •
tivist judge • actus reus • administrative law • admiralty law • agent • albatross • alimony • alternative pleading • amnesty • ambulance chaser • antitrust l
al • arbitrary and capricious • armed and dangerous • as is • assumpsit • attorney • b.m.w. • bad debt • bait and switch • bankrupt • bankruptcy • bar • bar r
se • basis • bench • best evidence rule • big gun • bilious • billable hour • birdie • black acre • black letter law • blue book • bogart • bogie • boiler plate • bo
• boot • booty • bork • bribe • bust • busted • c a f.o. • calendar call • chain • child support • churning the file • circumstantial evidence • citation • class ac
rly • clients • closing costs • coffee • comparative negligence • compensatory damages • consideration • constitutional law • contract • contributory neglige
umacious • corporation • corpus delicti • counselor • creditor • cross examination • dead file • dead man's acts • deceit • deep pocket • de minimis non curat
urrer • deposition • derogatory clause • devil's dictionary • dictionary, law • directed verdict • disclosure • divorce • dormant commerce clause • dorr's Rebel
le billing • double jeopardy • due process • dying declaration • e.s.o p. employee share ownership plan • eagle • economic development program • ego •
ndment • ejuration • entitlement • equal protection clause • equity • escheat • estate • estop • estoppel, equitable • ethics • evidence, laws of / rules of • e
ance • exclusionary rule • exculpatory evidence rule • exhaustion of remedies • ex-wife/ex-husband • face time • fair • fair use doctrine • fairway • false ar
ral judge • federalism • federal witness protection program • federalist society • fifth amendment • filibuster • first amendment • floating crap game • fourt
ndment • fourth amendment • force majeure • franking privilege • fraud • frivolous • fruit of the poisonous tree • fundamental right • garden • general denial •
der • gift causa mortis • gift tax • gloss • good samaritan statues • got my papers! • great compromise • graft • gross • guarantee clause • guilt • h.a.p. • h
us • habitability • habitability, warrantee of • hack • hand, Learned • harmless error • harvard law • hassle • hazardous • hazardous waste • headnote • hea
om • hereinabove, hereinafter, heretofore • he said, she said • homicide • hornbook • hose • hundred weight • hung jury • ill fame • immoral • impediment